HIDDEN PLAN

George Curle

*"God nothing does,
nor suffers to be done,
but we would do the same,
could we but see the events of time
as well as He"*

(Author Unknown)

New Wine Press

New Wine Press
P.O. Box 17
Chichester PO20 6YB
England

ISBN 0 947852 61 1

Printed in England by Clays Ltd, St Ives plc

Dedication

This book is dedicated to

ALL who

LOVE and LOOK

for His appearing -

whether they be of the

PRE, MID OR POST

TRIBULATION persuasion.

1 Timothy 6:14-16

Acknowledgments

The discoveries in this book would not have been made were it not for the labours of men in the past, in the fields of astronomy, chronology and Bible numerics, not forgetting present day scholars. I feel like a dwarf standing on the shoulders of these giants. They are referred to in the Select Biography, p.186.

I am also most grateful to my old friend, MRS PATRICIA GRYLLS for her as always enthusiastic and competent typing of the manuscript, ably assisted by MRS ROXANNE KRIJNEN and MRS JANE TWIZELL. Also to MRS EMILY ELLIS who graciously took time out on very short notice to proof-read the text.

A special word of thanks to MRS MURIEL WICKMAN and her home group. Their enthusiastic reception of these chronoprophetic lectures, and their prayerful concern has been a continuing source of encouragement.

Also to two Christian businessmen, PETER McERLANE, and KERRY O'MALLEY, who have supported me with sound advice and generous practical support.

We gratefully acknowledge folk around the world who have taken time out to write to us, after ''Times of the Signs'' was published. Their words of appreciation have greatly stimulated the writing of ''God's Hidden Plan'', above all - *to the LORD GOD who alone gives insight and understanding* (Daniel 9:22 Amos 3:7).

THE Holy SPIRIT

Preface

The phrase, "it is later than you think," has been on the lips of Christian spokesmen for many generations. Back in the 1940's the Christian public was confronted with God's clock which said it was five minutes to midnight. Since that generation time has ticked on to 11:59 p.m.

Many believers have been turned off the prophetic aspects of Scripture because of misinterpretations, wild speculations and date fixing for the Rapture. In the same home church where Mr. Curle and I were nurtured during the war years I heard preachers maintain during the course of World War II that Hitler was the Anti-christ, then Mussolini was given that distinction and finally Tojo the leader of Japan was afforded that designation. Since living in the U.S.A. I heard it spread far and wide that the respected Secretary of State, Henry Kissinger was the arch rival of the Lord.

However, in spite of the negative aspects of these well-meaning evangelical prophets we need to heed the teachings of the Bible and of Christ in particular concerning the end times. Other generations have sensed the nearness of the Lord, but surely the signs spelled out by the New Testament writers are manifested clearly today.

I first heard the author preach while he was still in his military uniform following his return to New Zealand at the end of the Second World War. His message then was one of urgency. Now, a generation later in his book "Times of the Signs," and the sequel, "God's Hidden Plan," the spirit of urgency has not waned.

What God has hidden from man is normally a challenge for man to seek it out. That is true in the area of nature and science as man, down through the ages, has discovered what God placed in the universe from the time of creation. If the moon, sun and stars were placed in the universe, as Mr Curle suggests, for some reason more than giving sunlight in the daytime and reflected light in the night then what is offered in this book should be required reading for the Christian public at large and non-Christians because of the many appeals throughout the book for the lost to come to grips with God's grace and salvation through Jesus Christ.

Two verses have come to my attention since reading "God's Hidden Plan." In I Peter 1:7 the big fisherman of Galilee declared that *"The end of all things is at hand"* (NIV). Since the day Jesus ascended His coming has been imminent. Although His delay has caused the critics to scoff and Christians to be sidetracked by materialism and secularism, nevertheless it is truer than ever, that the end of all things is at hand.

The second verse was spoken through the mouth of the prophet Jeremiah who acted as God's spokesman when he announced, *"I will hasten my word to perform it."* (KJV) Normally we do not think of God as being in a hurry, but if Mr Curle is right, based on scientific methodology and mathematical precision, then God will perform and fulfil His plan according to His timetable revealed in Scripture.

Since indeed the time is short, let us both "occupy until He returns" and at the same time, "look up for your salvation draws near."

Dr. Bernard Holmes
Southwest Baptist University
Bolivar, MO 65613
U.S.A.

Contents

The Secret Things Belong
To The Most High God
Those Things Revealed
    Belong To Us
The Holy Spirit Takes of The
Things of God And Reveals
Them To Us

The Hidden Plan

"I will give thee the treasures of darkness, and HIDDEN RICHES of SECRET PLACES". (Isaiah 45:3)

"Why, seeing TIMES are not HIDDEN from the Almighty, do they that know Him not see His days?" (Job 24:1)

"From now on I will tell you of NEW things, of HIDDEN things unknown to you". (Isaiah 46:6)

"He setteth an END to darkness ...... the thing that is HID bringeth He forth to light". (Job 28:3,11)

"If thou seekest her as silver, and searchest for her as for HID TREASURES; then shalt thou understand the fear of the Lord, and find the knowledge of God". (Proverbs 2:4-5)

"There is nothing covered, that shall not be revealed; and HID, that shall not be known". (Matthew 10:26)

"I thank Thee, O Father, Lord of heaven and earth, for that thou hast HID these things from the wise and prudent, and hast revealed them unto babes". (Luke 10:21)

"Praise be to the name of God for ever and ever ...... He reveals DEEP and HIDDEN things; He knows what lies in darkness, and LIGHT dwells with Him." (Dan. 2:27-28)

Introduction

This book, a sequel to "Times of the Signs" published in 1988, provides exciting new material confirming beyond all reasonable doubt that the return of the Lord Jesus Christ is *"near, right at the door"*

(Matthew 24:33-4).

We will see that there is a united fivefold witness warning us that this is the final decade before the Kingdom of God will be set up on earth. These witnesses whose timing converges in exact unison, are:-

1. Bible Chronology.
2. The Bible's surface meaning.
3. The Bible's hidden meaning in numerics.
4. The heavenly motions of the sun, earth and moon.
5. The timing of historical and current events.

In a world being convulsed with recurring disasters and endless, needless upheavals and bloodshedding, what peace of mind informed prophetic students have, as they learn more and more of God's governance of the past, present and future.

"The Lord foils the plans of the nations;
He thwarts the purposes of the peoples.
But the plans of the Lord stand firm forever,
The purposes of His heart through all generations".

(Psalm 33:10-11 NIV)

As one writer has well said, "when our thinking is in line with God's Program, then we shall see His hand in the TURMOIL around us, we shall escape the disappointment of the MIRING of the wheels of progress; and then we shall remain tranquil and in patience possess our souls in these solemn times". (And behold the camels were coming E.C. Kurtz.)

We wait in HOPE for the Lord;
He is our help and shield.
In Him our hearts rejoice,

xiii

for we trust in His holy name.
May your unfailing love rest
upon us, O Lord,
even as we put our HOPE in you.

(Psalm 33:20-20 NIV)

The threefold purpose of this book together with ''Times of the Signs'' is:-

(1) To WONDER AND WORSHIP God the creator, as we learn how He has planned and brought about the cyclic timed intervals of history.

(2) To be WARNED that the Lord Jesus Christ is about to return and take over the control of this planet.

(3) To be WON to Jesus Christ by the ministry of the Holy Spirit in the closing hours of this momentous age.

Chapter One

The Perfect Synchronization of History
History's Wonder Pattern
(Dia. 2 P.29)

When God decided to save Noah and his family from the corruption and violence that surrounded them, He gave them specific MEASUREMENTS for the ark:-

"And this is how you shall make it: the length of the Ark three-hundred cubits, its breadth fifty cubits, and its height thirty cubits." (Genesis 6:15 NKJV).

The tabernacle in the wilderness was to be built to very exacting MEASUREMENTS. The blue print, the pattern and the plan, the design, and all of its specifications were minutely made in heaven:-

"Let them make Me a sanctuary, that I may dwell among them. According to all that I show you, that is, the PATTERN of the tabernacle, and the PATTERN of all its furnishings, just so you shall make it."

(Exodus 25:8-9 NKJV).

In Ezekiel's vision of the millennial temple (chaps. 40:1-47:12) the word "MEASURE" or its equivalent occurs 63 times. The new Jerusalem is laid out to specific MEASUREMENTS:-

"And the one who spoke with me had a gold MEASURING ROD, to MEASURE the city, and its gates and its wall ..... and he MEASURED its wall, seventy-two yards according to human MEASUREMENTS, which are also angelic MEASUREMENTS." (Revelation 21:15-17 NASB).

15

Measured Time Predictions

Just as boats and buildings are built to specific MEASUREMENTS - so many Bible prophecies are predicted to occur after a specific TIME LAPSE, for example:-

"After seventy years ... I will visit you." (Jeremiah 29:10 NKJV). *"70 weeks are determined upon thy people and upon thy holy city."* (Daniel 9:24 NKJV). *"Destroy this temple, and I will raise it again in three days."* (John 2:19 NKJV).

Here is the shortest time lapsed prophecy in the Bible:-

"Jesus said to him, "Assuredly, I say to you that this very night, before the rooster crows, you will deny Me three times." (Matthew 26:34 NKJV).

Measured Time in History

Not only does God MEASURE boats, buildings, and chronological prophecies - but he has also locked specific historic events into exact MEASURED TIME SEQUENCES. In chapter four of 'Times of the Signs' I demonstrated the perfect time symmetry of history with nine events - dealing with the 'Times of the Temples' I said then, "In finding this bearing in December 1985 I felt more excited than Columbus sighting land; or Sir Edmund Hillary conquering Mt. Everest" so imagine my elation when I found not nine but eighteen historic occasions, perfectly synchronised into B.C. and A.D. events!

It's important at this stage to peruse Dia. 2 (p.29) before reading on - "one picture is worth a thousand words."

God at 'Sixes and Sevens'

The idiom "at sixes and sevens" conveys, to older readers at least, the thought of confusion, disorder, not knowing which way to turn. But with God we are going to see it means the exact opposite - order, harmony, synchronization. Taking key B.C. Jewish events whose years end with a six e.g. 586 The Fall of Jerusalem, we are going to find they perfectly synchronize, with no manipulation whatsoever into A.D. Jewish events whose years end with a seven e.g. 1967 the "Six Day War."

Step One B.C. 1846 Isaac Inherits

This is our basic date; it is amazing how much prophetic timing flows from this year. Bible chronology gives us exactly 400 years from this date to the Exodus which occured in 1446 B.C.

"And the child grew and was weaned, and on the day that Isaac was weaned, Abraham made a great feast."

(Genesis 21:8).

Isaac was the first Jew, born out of a miracle, and Jewish time officially started ticking when Ishmael was banished from Abraham's tents at the time Isaac was weaned. Isaac was actually born in B.C. 1951; trying to work chronoprophetic periods from his birth inevitably end in a stalemate. But working from B.C. 1846 marvellous patterns develop.

Step Two B.C. 1406 Israel
Enters Canaan

This 440 year time span becomes meaningful when we synchronize it later with its A.D. equivalent. The miraculous experience which enabled the Israelites to cross the river Jordan on dry land into the Promised Land is recorded in Joshua 3.

"The waters which came down from above stood and rose up upon a heap ... and those that came down toward the salt sea, failed, and were cut off, so the people passed over right against Jericho." (Joshua 3:16).

Step Three B.C. 966 Solomon's Temple Started

Amazingly enough we have another 440 year time span from their entering the Promised Land to the commencement of Solomon's Temple in B.C. 966:-

"In the four hundred and eightieth year after the children of Israel had come out of the land of Egypt (B.C. 1446) in the fourth year of Solomon's reign over Israel, in the month of Ziv, the second month, he began to build the house of the Lord." (1 Kings 6:1 NKJV)

Step Four B.C. 586 The Fall Of Jerusalem

From the start of Solomon's temple in B.C. 966 until that tragic year in Israel's history B.C. 586 is exactly 380 years. Incidentally if we add up all the measurements of the Ark 300 + 50 + 30 they equal exactly 380! There is no connection that I am aware of, - but I thought you might be interested.

"On the tenth day of the fifth month, in the nineteenth year (B.C. 586) of Nebuchadnezzar, King of Babylon, Nebuzaradan commander of the imperial guard, who served the King of Babylon, came to Jerusalem.

He set fire to the Temple of the Lord, the Royal Palace, and all the houses of Jerusalem, every important building he burned." (Jeremiah 52:12-13 NIV)

Step Five B.C. 566 Nebuchadnezzar's Insanity

According to Ussher, the King of Babylon became insane twenty years after the sacking of Jerusalem in B.C. 586. It is recorded in Daniel 4:25-27.

"You will be driven away from men, your dwelling shall be with the beasts of the field .... till you know that the Most High rules in the Kingdom of Men." (Daniel 4:25 NKJV).

Step Six B.C. 536 The Start Of The Second Temple

Cyrus, King of Persia, came to the throne in 538 B.C. (Thiele p.227 3rd edition) and according to Ezra 1:1-3 gave permission for the Jews to return and rebuild their temple. That year Zerubbabel led the first contingent of the exiles back to Jerusalem (Ezra chap. 1 & 2). Two years later, that is B.C. 536, they began building the second temple:-

"In the second month of the second year (B.C. 536) *of their coming to the house of God at Jerusalem, Zerubbabel .... laid the foundation of the Temple of the Lord."* (Ezra 3:8-10 NKJV).

Thus we have a 30 year time span (B C. 566-536) that will become very meaningful when we slot it into place shortly with A.D. events.

Step Seven B.C. 516 Completion Of Second Temple

20 years later after much opposition and many hassles the temple was finally completed in B.C. 516.

"They finished building the temple according to the commandment of the God of Israel, and according to the commandment of Cyrus, Darius and Artaxerxes Kings of Persia. (Ezra 6:14).

"The happy result was that the second temple was finished in 516 B.C. (Archer. Encyclopedia Bible Difficulties).

"They finished building the temple .... on the third day of adar (mid Feb-March) *in the sixth year of the reign of King Darius."* (Ezra 6:14-15).

Step 8 B.C. 486 Xerxes King Of Persia

Darius I died in B.C. 486 and that year King XERXES acceded to the Persian throne. This is the King who Esther married, and thus saved the Jewish nation from extermination. He is King Ahasuerus in the King James version, which is a Hebrew variant of Xerxes.

Thus from B.C. 516 to B.C. 486 we have our final B.C. time span of 30 years.

The Interlocking A.D. Events (Dia. 1)

In the diagram of a Yale key one can see how the serrations in the key must be correctly spaced apart to match the tumbler pins in the lock; no other key will unlock the door. Using the lock as an illustration of the B.C. events in Jewish history, we will learn how only ONE KEY in A.D. events perfectly matches the lock. I was out fishing one day with a London University Professor and I asked him this question "could he see any rhyme or reason in history? I will never forget the reply of this highly educated man "George, history is just a kaleidoscope of unrelated events." Let us now learn just how he was so very, very wrong.

Step 9 637 A.D. Omar Captures Jerusalem

We are now into the matching sevens of our B.C. sixes. In 637 A.D. Omar captured Jerusalem from the Romans who had occupied it intermittently since Pompey captured the city in B.C. 64 - an exact period of 700 years! (64 + 637 − 1 = 700). Refer to App. 5 if you have difficulty calculating from B.C. to A.D. dates.

In B.C. 1846 Ishmael, the father of the Moslems, was driven from Abraham's tent - now in 637 A.D. we find him pushing his nose into the tent once more. In Gibbon's Decline and Fall of the Roman Empire, we read:-

"Abu Obedia, the Mahommedan General laid seige to Jerusalem towards the close of 636 A.D. The city was then occupied by the Romans, who held out for four months. When they capitulated, the patriarch SOPHRONIUS obtained a clause in the treaty giving security to the inhabitants, and requiring the ratification

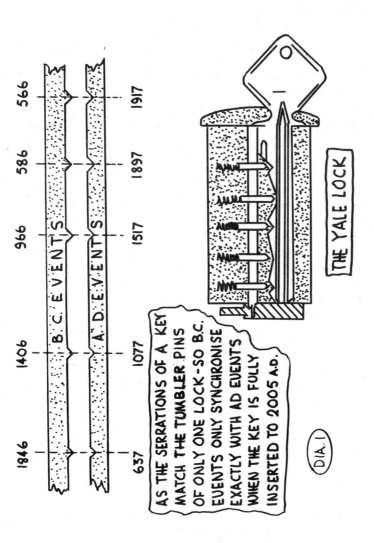

1846   1406   966   586   566

B.C. EVENTS

A.D. EVENTS

637   1077   1517   1897   1917

THE YALE LOCK

AS THE SERRATIONS OF A KEY
MATCH THE TUMBLER PINS
OF ONLY ONE LOCK - SO B.C.
EVENTS ONLY SYNCHRONISE
EXACTLY WITH AD EVENTS
WHEN THE KEY IS FULLY
INSERTED TO 2005 A.D.

DIA. 1

of OMAR himself. Omar who had to be sent for, arrived some six months afterwards, and the delay caused the actual delivering up of the city to take place early in the autumn of A.D. 637.''

Note ''A.D. 637 concerns only the city of Jerusalem. The Romans were not completely driven out from the land until Caesarea had fallen in 638, when the conquest was finally completed.'' Bullinger ''Witness of the Stars.'' ———

Step 10 A.D. 1077 The Seljuk Turks Seize Jerusalem

Matching the first 440 years in our ''B.C. Lock'' we come to the year A.D. 1077 for the second serration in our A.D. Key. ''In that year, the SELJUKS, a Turkish tribe, captured Jerusalem.'' (LANDAY - Dome of the Rock 1972).

''After A.D. 1000 the Seljuk Turks spread rapidly, creating the first Turkish Empire which lasted until the early 13th century. An event of enormous importance was their conversion to Islam in A.D. 960.

Malik Shah (1073-93) conquered Syria and Palestine. The Seljuks were by now extremely powerful and a great threat to Christian influence in the Middle East, but as new converts to Islam they were less tolerant than the Arabs. When they began to deny Christian pilgrims access to the Holy Places, Pope Urban III called for a crusade to free the Holy Land from the Saracens (as the Muslims were known). This led to a growing and bitter conflict between Christian Europe and the Muslim Middle East that was to last for centuries.'' (Datelines of World History - Gordon)

Step 11 A.D. 1517 Selim Captures Jerusalem

Matching the second 440 years in our ''B.C. Lock'' we come to the year A.D. 1517 for the third serration in our ''A.D. Key.''

"Jerusalem remained subject to the Mamlukes until 1517 A.D. when the Ottoman Sultan, Selim I, took it and inaugurated a Turkish regime, which was to last for exactly 400 years." (Enc Brittanica - Article on Jerusalem).

Step 12 A.D. 1897 First Zionist Congress

Matching the 380 year time span in our "B.C. Lock" our fourth serration in our "A.D. Key" fits perfectly into A.D. 1897.

Under the leadership of Theodore Herzl, on Sunday, August 29th 1897 the first Zionist Congress opened in Basle, Switzerland. For the first time in more than 1800 years, 196 delegates came from all over the world to openly discuss ways and means for the return to Zion.

What a vital, key date this year is to understanding chronophecy. It is exactly 1260 years from A.D. 637 when Omar captured Jerusalem, and 1900 years from the birth of Christ in B.C. 4 (4 + 1897 − 1 = 1900).

Step 13 A.D. 1917 The British Capture Jerusalem

Matching the first 20 years in our "B.C. Lock" we come to the year A.D. 1917 for the fifth serration in our "A.D. Key". When General Allenby, a born again Christian, with a young Lieutenant Montgomery (of later Alamein fame) captured Jerusalem - an air of expectancy and excitement was aroused throughout the Christian world. Prophetically informed Christians were aware that A.D. 1917 had been pinpointed from the previous century as a key crisis year for Israel. Grattan Guiness wrote in 1886 "There can be no question that those who live to see this year .... 1917 will have reached one of the most important .... of these terminal years of crisis (Light for the Last Days p.346). It was exactly 2520 years from the first year of Nebuchadnezzar's reign in 604 B.C. (2520 − 604 + 1 = 1917).

I have been told that as these Christian leaders of the British Army walked humbly on foot into Jerusalem on December 11 in 1917 they were all singing:-

"Jesus shall reign where'er the sun doth his successive journeys run; His Kingdom spread from shore to shore till moons shall wax and wane no more."

Soon, and very soon the Lord Jesus Christ will take over the rule and running of our sick, sin polluted world, when *"the government shall be on His shoulder; and of the increase of His government there shall be no end."*

Isaiah 9:6-7)

Then we shall truly sing:-
"Blessings abound where'er He reigns,
The prisoner leaps to loose his chains;
The weary find eternal rest,
And all the sons of want are blest.
Let every creature rise and bring,
Peculiar honours to our King;
Angels descend with songs again;
And earth repeat the loud amen!"

Step 14 A.D. 1947 U.N. Votes Israel Into A Nation

Matching the first 30 years in our "B.C. Lock" we come to the year A.D. 1947 for the sixth serration in our "A.D. Key."

What a momentous occasion for Israel! On the 29th November 1947 the General Assembly of the United Nations voted Israel a nation once more, with a foothold in Palestine their ancient homeland. This very date was pinpointed by Joseph's birth 1700 B.C.! See 'Times of the Signs' (pages 121-125).

Step 15 A.D. 1967 Israel Captures All Jerusalem

Matching the second 20 years in our "B.C. Lock" we come to the year 1967, for the seventh serration in our "A.D. Lock."

The 'six day war' in early June '67 proved to be a shattering and costly defeat for the Arabs. Egypt lost 260 aircraft on the ground in a pre-emptive dawn raid on the very first day of the war. In the Sinai desert they lost over 800 tanks. Thousands of Egyptians died - many of thirst as they roamed leaderless and lost in the desert areas of Sinai.

The Jordanian and Syrian fronts fared no better - over all the three fronts there were 689 Israelis killed to 13,500 Arabs. The capture of East Jerusalem and in particular the Wailing Wall and the Temple mount are of the greatest significance.

A.D. 1967 marks the beginning of the end of the Times of the Gentiles. Dr David Martyn Lloyd Jones, famed minister of Westminster Chapel, who generally played down any 'end time' prophetic teaching said at the time:-

"We are in a dissolving world. All my life I have opposed setting 'times and seasons' but I feel increasingly that we may be in the end times. What undergirds that conviction? To me A.D. 1967, the year the Jews occupied all of Jerusalem was very crucial. Luke 21:24 is one of the most prophetic verses. "Jerusalem", it reads, "*shall be trodden down of the Gentiles until the times of the Gentiles are fulfilled.*" It seems to me that that took place in 1967 - something crucially important that had not occurred in two thousand years." (Christianity Today).

An American prophetic author writing in October 1968 says :-

"As of June 1967, we must have entered a transitional period between the end of the present age and the beginning of the new age. The Bible demonstrates that eras in redemptive history do not abruptly end or suddenly begin. There was a transitional period between the Old and New Testament eras. We can expect such an interval between this present Church age and the coming Kingdom Age. It is quite apparent that we are in that interval." (A sign of Christ's Impending Advent. H.W. Butt)

I personally believe that the Times of the Gentiles began with a 40 year era from 626 – 586 B.C. and will end with another 40 year era A.D. 1967 - 2007. In 626 B.C. Nabopolasser became the first King of Babylon.

Elwood McQuaid in his excellent book "It is no Dream" says "We could well be witnessing the heralding of the beginning of the end. It is now clearly evident that since June 7, 1967 several important elements have ... become INTENSELY IDENTI-FIABLE." (Emphasis Mine p. 153)

Step 16 A.D. 1997 A Great Prophetic Crisis Year

I have written what I believe will occur in 1997 in chapter nine '1997 in chronophecy." But here we are showing that it is the terminal year of a historical pattern that has been steadily unfolding, slowly at first, but now with quickened tempo as the end of this incredible pattern draws near.

How privileged, how excited we should be as the end of a 3842 year pattern is now upon us! As the end of the age draws near we have been promised increased prophetic illumination of the revelation in Scripture. This promise in context (Daniel 12:9-12) is referring specifically to chronophecy. How many prophetic books are churned out each year monotonously reiterating what older writers wrote years ago!

"These words are CONCEALED and SEALED up till the time of the end." (Daniel 12:9)

If you want to discover and unseal the prophetic words of Scripture start digging in the fields of chronophecy. Grattan Guiness wrote in 1886 -

"Sacred chronology is no barren field to cultivate. The scriptures contain no unedifying statements, and they contain thousands of chronological ones! Has the church ever yet received from them any great comfort or consolation? Is not the time come that she should do so? Is she likely to do so without study? Has nature yielded to scientists her potent secrets without long and patient investigation and meditation? Are the material works of God more profound, and more worthy of research, than that WORD which is magnified above all HIS NAME (Psalm 138:2) which is "forever settled in heaven" - that word which is "truth" and which "liveth and abideth forever." A living thing has always something new in it; the Bible is no more exhausted than the rich storehouse of nature!

The very truths needed for our days of doubt and dark infidelity - new and glorious evidences of the inspiration of Scripture are there. Let us be hopeful and diligent, and seek to develop them for the glory of God." (Light for the Last Days p.222).

James Ramgay wrote in 1926:-

"Of this we are not, we cannot be, intended to remain in ignorance, for it is with regard to PROPHETIC CHRONOLOGY that it is expressly said - "the wise shall understand" (the End of the Age).

"May we be true "stewards of the mysteries of God" (1 Corinthians 4:1) and determine to say with Job "that which is with the Almighty I will not conceal." (Job 27:11)."

The Wonder Of This Pattern

At this stage we have seen fourteen dates in history interlocking to perfection, with only the last two to lock into place by 1997. One recent prophetic writer referring to the feast days of Israel's calendar says :-

"As we consider the critical importance of these prophetic events it is natural for us to enquire as to when it will all take place. Does the Bible give any indication of the time when these appointed events shall come to pass? The answer is a RESOUNDING

YES! As we look back over the history of our civilization's last four thousand years in the light of Scripture, we are confronted by a strange phenomenon. Despite the apparent random nature of historical dates and events, a curious pattern of astonishing complexity emerges when we examine the biblical prophecies regarding the nation of Israel and their precise fulfillment .... God's sovereignty over history and His foreknowledge are manifested clearly as He sets these prophetic appointments for Israel. Then as each time cycle concludes, He keeps the appointment by bringing the prophesied event to pass at the appointed time.

"Can any reasonable person believe that all of this has occurred simply by chance? It seems far more logical to this writer that we are observing an incredible display of God's sovereignty and that this phenomenon proves beyond a shadow of doubt that God truly has His hands on His Chosen People." (Armageddon G.R. Jeffrey p.10/159).

What is true of Israel's feast days is of course true of these interlocking B.C. and A.D. years.

"Have you not heard? Long ago I ordained it. In days of old I planned it; now I have brought it to pass."

(2 Kings 19:25 NIV)

2 KINGS 19=25

More Wonders Of This Incredible Plan (Dia. 2)

In chapter 4 "The 'S' FACTOR, we will show some of the wonders of the number SEVENTEEN, and how it is inextricably woven into Jewish chronology. We will also explain the meaning of 17:-

"God assuring us on oath that the complete cycle of events He has ordered will be perfectly accomplished."

This number seventeen pervades our lock and key design. The B.C. years in the lock 1846 - 486 cover a span of 1,360 years which is 17 x 80 years. Likewise the A.D. years in the key (637 - 1997) is another 1360 years or 17 x 80 years. If we measure from start to finish (B.C.

28

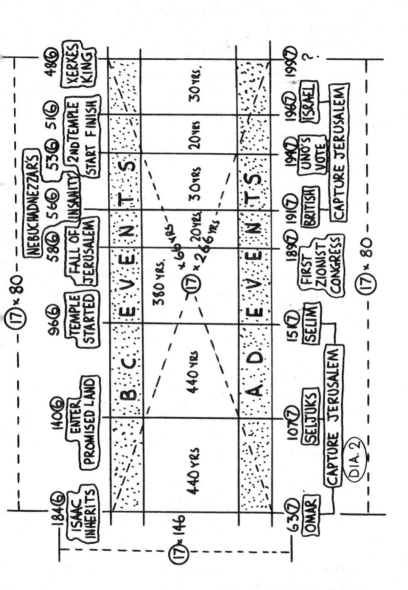

29

1846 to 1997 A.D.) we have a time span of 1846 + 1997 − 1 = 3842 years, which is exactly 17 x 226 years.

From the end of the B.C. lock B.C. 486 to the beginning of the A.D. Key 637 A.D. is 486 + 637 − 1 = 1122 years, which is exactly 17 x 66 years.

There are eight matching couplets in our B.C./A.D. pattern e.g. B.C. 1846 to 637 A.D. or B.C. 966 to 1517 A.D. If we add these coupling years together, every one of the eight adds up exactly to 2,482 years e.g. 1846 + 637 − 1 = 2,482. Now 2,482 years is exactly 17 x 146 years. Eight of these coupled years gives us 8 x 146 or 1168 seventeens!

1620 Seventeens

If we look at Dia. 2 we can see at a glance that these happenings in history did not just happen. They are not as my London professor friend declared -

"A mere kaleidescope of unrelated events"

If we look at these crisis years LONGITUDINALLY we find two 17 x 80 year cycles. If we look at them LATITUDINALLY we see eight 17 x 146 year cycles. If we look at them DIAGONALLY there is one of 17 x 226 year cycles, and one of 17 x 66 year cycles. Thus the total number of SEVENTEENS are :-

LONGITUDINALLY	2 x 80	= 160
LATITUDINALLY	8 x 146	= 1168
DIAGONALLY	1 x 226	= 226
	1 x 66	= 66
	Total	1620

1620 = 12 x 9 x 5 x 3. On giving these numbers their spiritual significance we could say - Here is the God-head (3) acting through grace (5) to bring to a conclusion (9) this marvellous plan by Divine administration (12).

Design Not Chance

As we see all these historical events perfectly synchronised, intertwined, and locked into each other over 3,842 years, one is tempted to show the mathematical probability of them happening by the laws of chance. The only problem with that approach is there are so many zeros in the answer that they exceed the mind's comprehension. I prefer to express it in a more down to earth way. If one cannot see God's incredible design and plan in His perfect synchronisation of history then as my Australian cousin would say -

"One must have Kangaroos in their top paddock!"

Extending the Wonder Pattern (Dia. 3)

We have seen a complete pattern connected with Jewish history culminating in 1997 A.D. But after this I believe we are to see the era of the Great Tribulation described by Jesus Christ as a period of *"great distress, unequalled from the beginning of the world until now - and never to be equalled again."* (Matthew 24:21)

If we extend eight years on to our 486 B.C. date we come to 478 B.C. This was a key year for Israel, Persia, and Babylon; Esther became the queen of Persia that year, and because of her position saved the Jewish nation from extermination through the Hitler of her day - Haman.

According to Leon Wood in "A Survey of Israel's History" 478 B.C. is the year King Xerxes destroyed Babylon, and melted down its gold idols - to pay for his expensive wars with the Greeks.

The A.D. year that would synchronise with this pattern is 2005!, the terminus ad quem of the 'Times of the Gentiles' as explained in my earlier book 'Times of the Signs.'

Now the longitudinal time spans on this extended pattern are 1368 years (1846 - 478) and (637 - 2005). Now

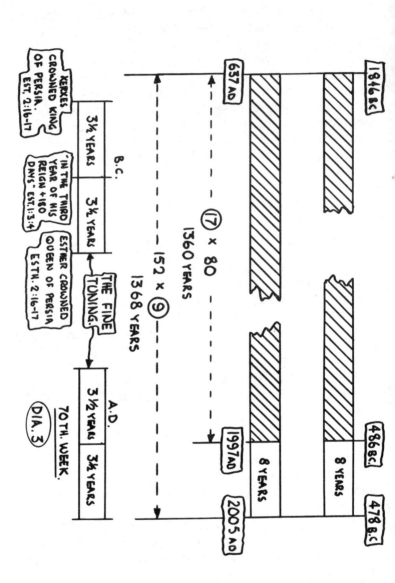

XERXES CROWNED KING OF PERSIA. EST. 2:16-17

3½ YEARS

B.C.

"IN THE THIRD YEAR OF HIS REIGN" +180 DAYS" EST.1:3:4

3½ YEARS

ESTHER CROWNED QUEEN OF PERSIA ESTH. 2:16-17

THE FINE TUNING.

A.D.

3½ YEARS   3¼ YEARS

70 TH. WEEK.

DIA. 3

637 AD

1846 B.C.

⑰ × 80
1360 YEARS

152 × ⑨
1368 YEARS

1997 AD

2005 AD

8 YEARS

486 B.C.

478 B.C.

8 YEARS

32

no longer is the span divisible by 17 - instead it is perfectly divisible by 9 (152 x 9 = 1368) this is the number that expresses JUDGMENT, FINALTY, THE CONCLUSION of a matter. See 'THE J FACTOR' in Times of The Signs.

The Fine Tuning

Plotting back seven 360 day years (70th Week of Daniel appendix two) from 2005 A.D. gives us the start of the Tribulation period. Can we match this in B.C. with some definite event seven years before 478 B.C.? We learn in Esther 2:16-17 that Esther was crowned Queen "in the seventh year of his reign."

The Super Fine Tuning

We know that 1260 days into the Tribulation Antichrist will break off his covenant with the Jews (Appendix 2 Times of the Signs). Can we find a similar time span in our B.C. 'lock'? In Esther 1:3 we read *"in the third year of his reign he gave a banquet for all his officials and servants."* (NKJV). A Persian year consisted of 360 days - so we have 3 x 360 = 1080 days; but we need 1260 days, if the key is going to match the lock. In the next verse we read *"for a full 180 days he displayed the vast wealth of his Kingdom and the splendor and glory of his majesty"* (v.4) So we have 1080 + 180 = 1260 days - precise, exact, perfect correspondence to the VERY DAY!

Job, after a deeply abasing experience, bowed down and acknowledged the sovereignty of God saying, *"I know that you can do all things, no plan of yours can be thwarted."* (Job 42:2 NIV)

Truly as we meditate on these fabulous facts in history our hearts must be drawn out in praise to an all-powerful, all-knowing heavenly father. *"O Lord you are my God; I will exalt you and praise your name, for in perfect faithfulness you have done marvellous things, things planned long ago."* (Isaiah 25:1 NIV)

Dr. Charles C. Ryrie has well said "God is not still on the throne. He is very active on that throne." Clarence Mason in his book on 'Prophetic Problems' says, "Do you really believe God is on a throne? Then quiet your fears! Someone who has power and wisdom is in on the case. He is not biting His fingernails, uneasily sitting on the edge of His throne, wondering what is going to happen and fearing that it will. He is in control! There is a throne and God is on it, as we read, *"The Lord hath prepared His throne in the heavens; and His Kingdom ruleth over all."* (Psalm 103:19)

Chapter Two

"The Abomination of Desolation"
(Dia. 4)

The last seven years of this age is known as the 70th week of Daniel. It is made up of seven years of 360 days each, giving us a total of 2520 days or two halves of 1260 days each. We saw in the 'waypoints' of 'Times of the Signs' that these time spans have had a prophetic significance in 'years' of 365.24 days e.g. From the rise of Babylon in 624 B.C. until Omar captures Jerusalem in 637 A.D. is 1260 solar years, and from 637 A.D. another 1260 years brings us to 1897 A.D. - the first Zionist Congress year!

In Daniel 12:11-12 we have two more time factors mentioned viz:- 1290 days and 1335 days. These of course are to be fulfilled as extensions in 'days' of the last half of the 70th week. (Matthew 29:15, 2 Thessalonians 2:4) Now just as the 1260 days also worked out in years likewise we find a perfect pattern when we convert the 1290 and 1335 days into years.

Knowledge "Sealed Until The Last Days"

Knowledge of these time spans was to be *"concealed and sealed up until the end time"* (Daniel 12:4,9) *"None of the wicked would understand, but the instructors* (Rotheram, NASB Margin) *who have insight will understand."* (Daniel 12:10)

The Amplified Bible conveys the true meaning of verse four :- *"But you, O Daniel, shut up the words and seal the book until the time of the end. Then many shall run to and fro and search anxiously through the Book, and knowledge of God's purposes as revealed by His prophets shall be increased and become great.''*

"Many shall run to and fro." Metaphorically the phrase means "to read through earnestly and thoroughly." (Speakers Commentary) This does not refer to trains, motor cars, boats and aeroplanes! The real sense is :- "Many shall peruse the book" (Variorum) "Many shall diligently investigate" (Darby) "Many shall read and review the book" (Pierson) "Many shall scrutinize the book from end to end." (Tregelles) "Many shall search it through and through" (Pember) and so "knowledge (of it) shall be increased.''

All the standard commentaries on Daniel freely acknowledge their lack of knowledge on these time spans of 1290 and 1335. For instance John Walvoord in his excellent commentary on Daniel says on page 292 :- "There is also the intimation that the ceaseless search for knowledge by men will go unrewarded either because they do not look for it, or because their time and circumstances does not justify their understanding of prophecy that does not immediately concern them. No doubt, those LIVING IN THE TIME OF THE END WILL HAVE FAR GREATER UNDERSTANDING OF THESE THINGS THAN IS POSSIBLE TODAY." (Emphasis mine).

The Light Dawns

For over 22,000 hours now, I have been searching diligently through God's Word, investigating its chronological data, especially as it refers to the End Times. Several have asked me about the 1290 and 1335 days of Daniel 12, and my only answer had been the standard viewpoint that it refers to days extending beyond the 1260 days of "Jacob's trouble" which of course is true, and is the primary meaning. However, in February 1990 the Holy Spirit quickened my understanding and showed me there is a foreshadowing fulfilment in 'years', of what will be literal 'days' in the final 70th week of Daniel. (Daniel 9:27, Matthew 24:15, 2 Thessalonians 2:4, Revelation 11:2)

We read in Daniel 12:11 *"From the time that the regular sacrifice is abolished, and the abomination of desolation is set up, there will be 1290 days."*

Rotheram puts it this way:- *"From the time of the taking away of the continual ascending sacrifice, and the placing of the horrid abomination that astoundeth shall be 1290 days."*

Well, the daily sacrifice was abolished initially when Solomon's temple was destroyed in 586 B.C. If we convert 1290 'days' into prophetic 'years' (as per Ezekiel 4:6, Numbers 14:34) we have $1290 \times 360 \div 365 = 1272.32$ years or $1290 \times 360 \div 365.24 = 1271.49$ years the mean average being 1271.90 or 1272 nearest number. I added 1272 years (solar) to 586 B.C. thus:- $1272 - 586 + 1 = 687$ A.D. That year meant nothing to me, it had never cropped up in all my previous studies. My encyclopedias of dates only referred to "Cuthbert at Lindisfarne. Pepin II subdued Neusteria and united the whole Frankish kingdom." What on earth did they have to do with the "setting up of the abomination of desolation?" A disappointing nothing at all!

The Dome Of The Rock

Then one day whilst reading "DOME OF THE ROCK" by Jerry M. Landay, Newsweek New York, I stumbled across this year 687 A.D. On pages 66 - 67 we read:- "To lure the faithful to Jerusalem the Caliph would mobilise the most able Byzantine and Persian architects and artisans in his empire and command them to create a shrine to shelter As-Sakhra (the sacred stone on the Temple Mount) that would be unsurpassed for sheer magnificence not only in all the Islamic world but in the empire of the Christian infidels of Constantinople as well .... He subsequently issued an edict forbidding his subjects to make the pilgrimage to Mecca. Jerusalem, "is now appointed for you instead...."

It was absolutely vital to Abd-al-Malik's scheme that

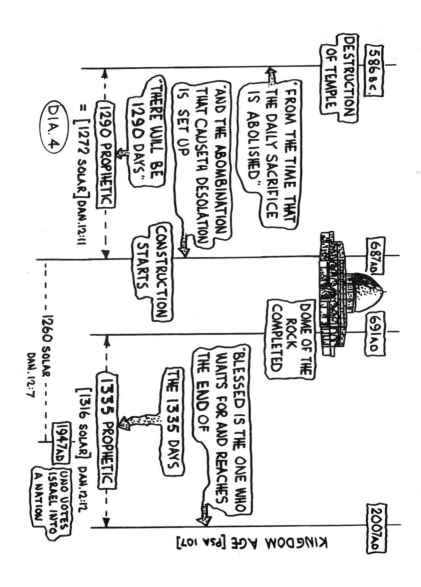

DIA. 4

586 B.C. — DESTRUCTION OF TEMPLE

'FROM THE TIME THAT THE DAILY SACRIFICE IS ABOLISHED'

'AND THE ABOMINATION THAT CAUSETH DESOLATION IS SET UP'

'THERE WILL BE 1290 DAYS'.

1290 PROPHETIC = [1272 SOLAR] DAN. 12:11

CONSTRUCTION STARTS

687 A.D.

DOME OF THE ROCK COMPLETED

691 A.D.

1260 SOLAR DAN. 12:7

1335 PROPHETIC [1316 SOLAR] DAN. 12:12

THE 1335 DAYS

'BLESSED IS THE ONE WHO WAITS FOR AND REACHES THE END OF'

1947 A.D. UNO VOTES ISRAEL INTO A NATION

2007 A.D.

KINGDOM AGE [PSA 107]

38

the Dome of the Rock not only be built well, but quickly. CONSTRUCTION BEGAN IN 687 A.D., and the structure was finished and dedicated only four years later in 691 A.D."

So from 586 B.C. adding 1290 prophetic years (1272 solar) we find in 687 A.D. "the placing of the horrid abomination that astoundeth" (Rotherham). On the very spot where Abraham offered up Isaac and God's temple once stood there now stands the Moslem Dome of the Rock. On the inside of the Dome there are 235 metres of inscriptions from the Koran denying that Jesus is the Son of God. The Koran is divided into 114 chapters called Suras. Here are some from inside the dome. Sura 5 verse 172. "O you Christian people of the Bible, do not exceed the limits of your faith, say nothing but the truth. The Messiah, the son of many, was only a messenger of Allah .... therefore do not declare that God is three."

Sura 19 verses 34 - 36
"This is the truth of Jesus son of Joseph, son of Mary, ... It does not befit Allah that he should take a son."
Another one reads :-
"If you will cease declaring so it will be better for you, for Allah is only one, glory to him. He is far from needing a son, for all that is in the earth and sky belongs to him ...."

So for 1300 years there has stood a building on the holy Temple site emphatically denying that Jesus is the Son of God! The Bible says :- *"who is the liar but the one who denies that Jesus is the Christ? This is the antichrist, the one who denies the FATHER AND THE SON."* (1 John 2:22)

No wonder the Crusaders called the Dome of the Rock - THE ABOMINATION OF DESOLATION!

The 1335 Days

"Blessed is the one who waits for and reaches the end of the 1,335 days" (Daniel 12:12 NIV).

We have seen that the 1290 days make sense when we

convert them into prophetic years and measure from the destruction of the Temple in 586 B.C. To be consistent let us convert the 1335 days into prophetic years :- 1335 x 360 ÷ 365.24 = 1316 years.

The Dome of the Rock was completed in 691 A.D. Adding 1316 years we come exactly to 2007 A.D. - the commencement of the glorious millennial reign of Christ on earth, when our prayers will be truly answered *"Thy Kingdom come, Thy will BE DONE ON EARTH as it is in Heaven."* (Matthew 6:10)

How *"blessed"* will be the one who *"reaches the end of the 1335 days!"* (Daniel 12:12 NIV)

The Significance Of The Temples

We have seen in the 'Symmetry of the Temples' (Times of the Signs) and 'The Abomination of Desolation' what a strategic place The Dome of the Rock holds in the planning of God. The first temple was built by a son of Isaac: Herod's temple was built by a son of Esau and now the Dome of the Rock built by a son of Ishmael!

Solomon's temple came to an ignominious end when in 586 B.C. *"they set fire to God's temple"* (2 Chronicles 36:15-16) the reason - *"The Lord God of their fathers, sent warnings to them by His messengers because he had compassion on His people and on His dwelling place. But they mocked God's messengers, despised His words and scoffed at His prophets until the wrath of the Lord arose against his people, till there was no remedy."* (2 Chronicles 36:15-16 NIV).

Herod's temple likewise was totally destroyed by the Roman Army in A.D. 70 because of the persistent unbelief of the Jewish nation that Jesus was the Son of God. (Matthew 23:37-38, 24:1-2, John 1:11, 19:7)

Likewise the Dome of the Rock with its blatantly inscribed denials that Jesus is the SON OF GOD is marked out for dramatic destruction. *"For a little while your people possessed your holy place, but now our enemies have trampled down your sanctuary ... Oh, that you would rend the heavens and come down ... our holy and glorious*

40

temple where our fathers praised you, has been burned with fire, and all that we treasured lies in ruins. After all this, O Lord, will you hold yourself back? (Isaiah 63:18, 64:1,11 NIV)

Chapter Three

The Perfect Balance Of History
(Dia. Nos. 5 - 10)

When we plotted out the "Times of the Temples" in "Times of the Signs" (pgs 45 - 66) we found that the year the Dome of the Rock was completed, 691 A.D. was the central year in the perfect symmetry of history. How crucial, how important, how pivotal 691 A.D. is in God's timing can be seen at a glance in Dia. No. 6.

Using the Moslem symbol, the crescent moon, which surmounts the Dome of the Rock as a fulcrum, we can see how God has perfectly balanced key B.C. dates with Jewish events since 1897 A.D. We read in Ezekiel 5:5 :- *"This is what the Sovereign Lord says: This is Jerusalem, which I have set in the CENTRE of the Nations. (NIV)"* The spiritual centre of Jerusalem is of course the Temple Mount. Just as Jerusalem is the GEOGRAPHICAL centre of the Nations, and the Temple Mount is the spiritual EPICENTRE of Judaism and Islam, so 691 A.D. is the CHRONOLOGICAL CENTRE of God's purposes, between the seed of Ishmael who built the Dome of the Rock, and the seed of Isaac who constructed Solomon's temple.

The light graceful arches facing the sides of the Dome at the top of the steps leading up to it, are known as MAWASIN i.e. scales. The belief is that on judgment day the souls of Moslems will be weighed in them.

Completion Of Second Temple (Dia. 5)

The second temple built after the Jews had returned from Babylon was completed in 516 B.C. (Ezra chapters

43

3 - 6 (see also "Times of the Signs" p. 50). Measuring from 516 B.C. to our fulcrum 691 A.D. we have a time span of 1206 years (516 + 691 − 1 = 1206). Extending 1206 years on from 691 A.D. we come to 1897 A.D. The great prophetic year of the FIRST ZIONIST CONGRESS - and so with all five of these B.C. time spans, they all are perfectly balanced with A.D. time spans culminating in a key prophetic year; reaching a climax in 2007 A.D., the beginning of the Kingdom age (Time of the Signs p. 195).

The Chronoprophetic Balancing Act (Dia. Nos. 7 - 10)

It might make it a little clearer to visualise it as 20, 30, 20, 40 year "weights" all balanced at the ends of the chronoprophetic see-saw! So we can see that historic B.C. events are perfectly balanced with prophetic A.D. events. Surely, *"honest scales and BALANCES are from the Lord - all the weights in the bag are of HIS MAKING."*
(Proverbs 16:11 NIV)

More Incredible Facts

These time spans are not just haphazard lengths of years - they are all connected with specific time scales in the Bible and amazingly with the orbits of the sun, earth and moon. Take for example the last span of 1316 years, how is that related to Scripture and astronomy? In Daniel 12:12 we have a time unit of 1335 days, which of course can be expanded scripturally to 1335 years (Ezekiel 4:6 & Numbers 14:34). If we call these 1335 prophetic years (360 days per annum) they equal 1316 solar years - 1335 x 360 ÷ 365.24 = 1316! In Daniel Chapter Twelve we have three cryptic figures 1.1260, 2.1290 and 3.1335.

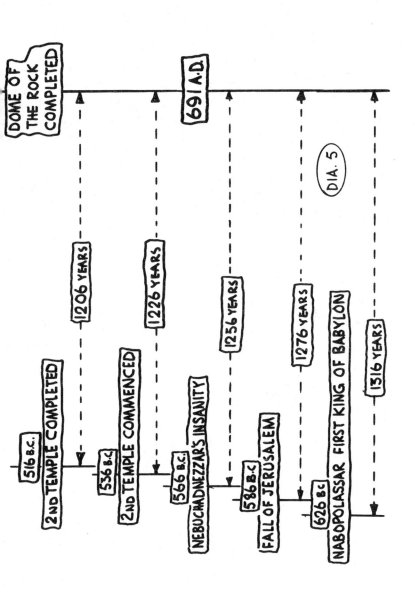

DIA. 5

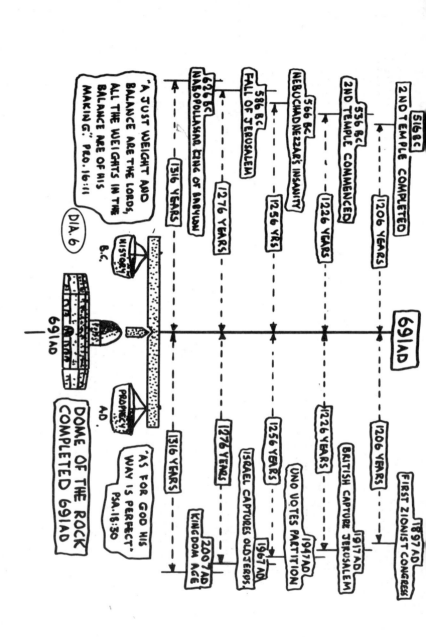

DIA. 6

"A JUST WEIGHT AND BALANCE ARE THE LORDS; ALL THE WEIGHTS IN THE BALANCE ARE OF HIS MAKING." PRO. 16:11

"AS FOR GOD HIS WAY IS PERFECT." PSA. 18:30

DOME OF THE ROCK COMPLETED 691AD

691 AD

B.C.   HISTORY   691AD   PROPHECY   A.D.

B.C. side (top):
- 625 BC NABOPOLLASAR KING OF BABYLON
- 586 BC FALL OF JERUSALEM
- 566 BC NEBUCHADNEZZAR'S INSANITY
- 536 BC 2ND TEMPLE COMMENCED
- 516 BC 2ND TEMPLE COMPLETED

- 1316 YEARS
- 1276 YEARS
- 1256 YRS
- 1226 YEARS
- 1206 YEARS

A.D. side (bottom):
- 1316 YEARS
- 1276 YEARS
- 1256 YEARS
- 1226 YEARS
- 1206 YEARS

- 2007 AD KINGDOM AGE
- 1967 AD ISRAEL CAPTURES OLD JERUS.
- 1947 AD UNO VOTES PARTITION
- 1917 AD BRITISH CAPTURE JERUSALEM
- 1897 AD FIRST ZIONIST CONGRESS

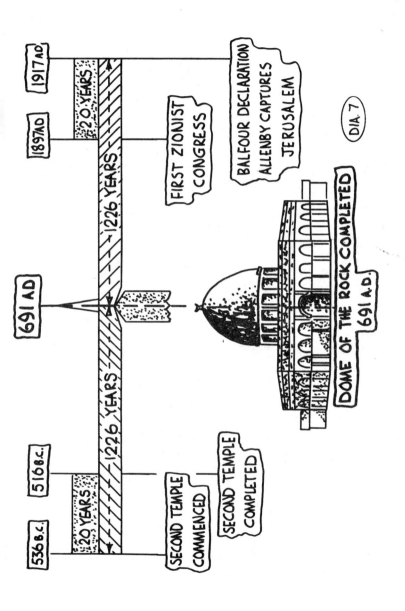

536 B.C. | 516 B.C. | 691 AD | 1897 AD | 1917 AD

20 YEARS

1226 YEARS

1226 YEARS

20 YEARS

SECOND TEMPLE COMMENCED

SECOND TEMPLE COMPLETED

DOME OF THE ROCK COMPLETED 691 A.D.

FIRST ZIONIST CONGRESS

BALFOUR DECLARATION
ALLENBY CAPTURES JERUSALEM

DIA. 7

47

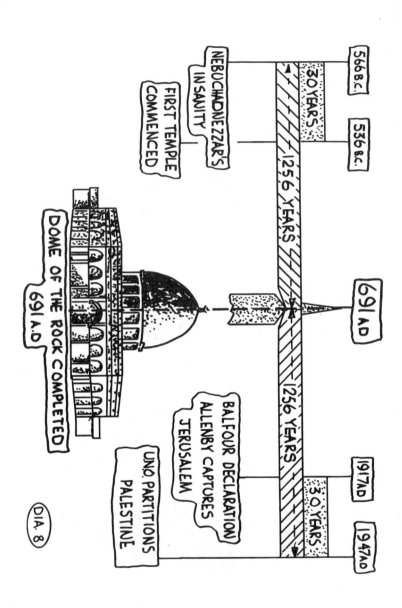

NEBUCHADNEZZAR'S INSANITY

FIRST TEMPLE COMMENCED

566 B.C.

536 B.C.

30 YEARS

1256 YEARS

DOME OF THE ROCK COMPLETED 691 A.D.

691 A.D.

1256 YEARS

BALFOUR DECLARATION ALLENBY CAPTURES JERUSALEM

U.N.O. PARTITIONS PALESTINE

1917 A.D.

1947 A.D.

30 YEARS

DIA. 8

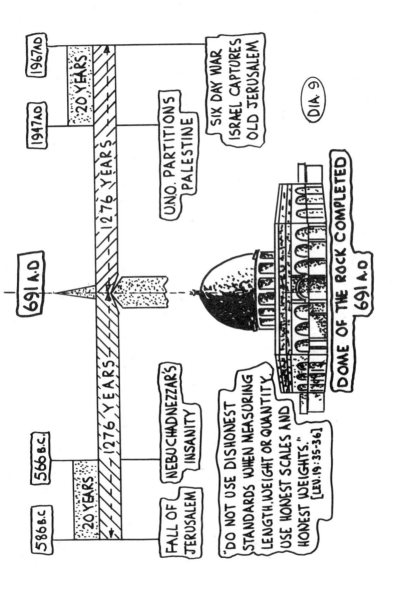

586 B.C.   566 B.C.   691 A.D   1947AD   1967AD

20 YEARS   20 YEARS

1276 YEARS   1276 YEARS

FALL OF JERUSALEM

NEBUCHADNEZZAR'S INSANITY

U.N.O. PARTITIONS PALESTINE

SIX DAY WAR ISRAEL CAPTURES OLD JERUSALEM

"DO NOT USE DISHONEST STANDARDS WHEN MEASURING LENGTH, WEIGHT OR QUANTITY. USE HONEST SCALES AND HONEST WEIGHTS." [LEV. 19:35-36]

DOME OF THE ROCK COMPLETED 691 A.D

(DIA. 9)

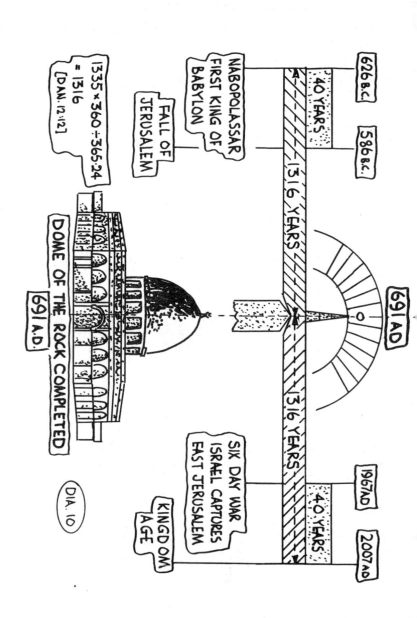

NABOPOLASSAR
FIRST KING OF
BABYLON

FALL OF
JERUSALEM

1335 × 360 ÷ 365·24
= 1316
[DAN. 12:12]

626 B.C.

40 YEARS

586 B.C.

1316 YEARS

DOME OF THE ROCK COMPLETED

691 A.D.

691 A.D.

0

1316 YEARS

SIX DAY WAR
ISRAEL CAPTURES
EAST JERUSALEM

1967 A.D.

40 YEARS

2007 A.D.

KINGDOM
AGE

DIA. 10

1335 and Astronomy

One prophetic writer wrote in 1969 - "The third cryptic figure is 1335 days. This one is the most significant of all. It predicts a time of blessedness as foretold by the angel. But where does this number come from? This number more than any other I know proves that the great Creator of the universe is also one who wove into the timing of the prophetic periods of Israel's history this astronomical figure. This period of 2520 years of Gentile dominion over Israel contains seventy five cycles of thirty three years, in each of which the sun gains on the moon one solar year. Seventy five of these cycles add up to 2,475 years, and this exceeds 2,520 lunar years by thirty years, and falls short of 2520 solar years by forty-five. This astronomical calculation shows that 2520 lunar years come short of 2520 solar years by seventy-five years.

"Now the number 1290 is obtained by adding this thirty years by which the seventy five cycles exceed 2520 lunar years to the number 1260. Then the number 1335 is obtained by adding seventy five years, the difference between the 2520 lunar and 2520 solar years, to that same number 1260. Only He who created these rolling spheres and set the timings of the orbits of the moon around the earth, and the earth around the sun could possibly know and work into these prophetic calculations such evidences of His handiwork in creation. To me this brings the glory of God into the prophetic word of Him who orders and controls all the universe and all the movements in human history to the end of time." (Windows on Jerusalem p.64 Dr. W.G. Hathaway).

This number 1335 will crop up again in chapter eleven, The Tents of Abraham, as it has already in chapter 2 The Abomination of Desolation.

1276 And 1256 Years

The next two time spans 1276 and 1256 are also

connected to the Bible's prophetic time scales. We learnt in 'The Times of the Gentiles' that the span is not 2520 years, but 2590 years, which is 37 x 70. In chapter 7 we learn that 37 is the unique numeric number for Jesus Christ, and of course 70 is the basic measuring scale in Scripture. Now just as 2520 and its half 1260 are used in Scripture, so, 2590 of Ezekiel 4 and Leviticus 26 has a half number of 1295. Now 1295 prophetic years are 1295 x 360 ÷ 365.24 which equals 1276 years!

Now to obtain the 1256 years that sea-saw through to 1947 A.D. we simply multiply the 1296 by lunar years which are 354.36 days, 1295 x 354.36 ÷ 365.24 = 1256 solar years.

The other figures are also connected with the timing of the earth and moon - but the calculations are too complicated for the general reader - guess your head is swimming enough already!

Psalm 89:19-37 reaffirms the COVENANT to David that his throne will endure FOREVER and the climax of all the beautiful promises in these verses is :- *"his throne will be established forever like the MOON, the faithful witness in the sky."* (v. 37 NIV). How faithfully the moon with scripture and history are witnessing since 1897 A.D. that by 2007 A.D. the Davidic throne will be established on earth. *"The moon marks off the seasons"* (Psalm 104:19). This pattern is perfect because it came from the Divine drawing board.

Moses sings:- *"Oh praise the greatness of our God .... His works are PERFECT."* (Deuteronomy 32:4)

David sings:- *"as for God, his way is PERFECT"* (Psalm 18:30 NIV).

John tells us that with Jesus Christ *"through him all things were made - nothing was made that has been made"* (John 1:3 NIV) and that includes chronophecy! So with utmost, abounding confidence *"Let us fix our eyes on Jesus, the author and the PERFECTER of our faith."*
(Hebrews 12:2 NIV)

Another Historic/Prophetic Balance

In 616 B.C. the Babylonian viceroy Nabopolassar revolted against the Assyrian rule in Nineveh. That is 1306 years before 691 A.D. To balance the scale we add on 1306 years to 691 A.D. - and it comes to 1997 A.D.! Surely a coming critical crisis year in prophecy.

Chapter Four

The 'S' Factor

When one purchases a different make of car, one suddenly becomes aware and perhaps surprised how many models of that particular car there are on the road. A student of landscape painting develops an ever increasing perception of the colours, the beauty and the tones of nature all around, and so the illustration could be multiplied ad-infinitum.

Likewise with the chronological data in the Bible, the deeper it is studied, the more heightened becomes the awareness of the significance of numbers and dates. The prophet Haggai says :- *"Now give careful thought from this day on, consider how things were ... From this day on, from this twenty-fourth day of the ninth month, give careful thought to the day when the foundation of the Lord's temple was laid."* (Haggai 2:15-18 NIV)

The word of the Lord came to Ezekiel :- *"Son of Man, record this DATE, this VERY DATE because the King of Babylon has laid seige to Jerusalem THIS VERY DAY."* (Jan 15th 588 B.C.) (Ezekiel 24:2 NIV)

Throughout the Bible dates abound in YEARS and in many cases the actual month and sometimes the VERY DAY is recorded:-

"In the NINTH YEAR, in the TENTH MONTH, on the TENTH DAY, the word of the Lord came to me ...." (Ezekiel 24:1 NIV)

Have you given, as the Scriptures exhort, *"careful thought"* to the numbers and dates in the Bible? When one perceives the significance of the meaning of Bible numbers, and learns of the marvellous patterns in the time cycles of history, astronomy and the Bible, these once dry, boring areas of the Bible suddenly become alive with wonder, beauty and purpose like flowers bursting forth after rain on drought stricken land - the more so *"as we see THE DAY approaching."* (Hebrews 10:25)

In Chapter ten of "Times of the Signs" we learnt about the importance of the numbers 9 and 19 in the "J" factor - they are given numbers of judgment, horror and destruction. Lets now find the saccharinity of chronophecy, or honey if you prefer. In the number SEVENTEEN we will discover the "S" factor, the sweetness, the pleasantness, the honeydew, that awaits the redeemed of the Church and the remnant of Israel.

In Genesis 7:11 we read:-

"In the six hundredth year of Noah's life, on the SEVENTEENTH day of the second month - on that day all the springs of the great deep burst forth, and the floodgates of the heavens were opened." (NIV)

Our God takes special care to inform us that it was on the SEVENTEENTH day that the floodwaters of judgment came on the earth. On that day Noah and his family were safe in the Ark. *"On that very DAY .... The Lord shut him in"* (7:13,16 NIV). Noah was SAFE. Noah was secure. He could fall over in the Ark, but it was impossible for him to fall overboard! Likewise every believer in CHRIST is safe for eternity :-

"Therefore there is now no condemnation for those who are in Christ Jesus" (Romans 8:1) *"Ye are SEALED unto the day of redemption".* (Ephesians 4:30)

The flood waters of judgment for our sins fell on Jesus Christ on the cross. In God's reckoning Christians are reckoned to be "IN HIM". Then, we were :-

	1. Crucified together with Christ	Gal. 2:20
	2. Died together with Christ	Col. 2:20
	3. Buried together with Christ	Rom. 6:4
	4. Quickened together with Christ	Eph. 2:5
	5. Raised together with Christ	Col. 3:1
We are	6. Sufferers together with Christ	Rom. 8:17
We will be	7. Glorified together with Christ	Rom. 8:17

How sweet is the "S" factor of SEVENTEEN! In Genesis 8:4 we read:- *"On the SEVENTEENTH day of the seventh month the Ark came to rest on the mountains of Ararat."* (NIV)

This word REST in Hebrew means "to rest, to sit down." (Gesenius Lexicon). On the 17th day the Ark rested, or sat down, as soon as the judgment waters had subsided, leaving Noah safe on the other side of the flood. How this vividly pictures for us the Lord Jesus - *'"But this man, after He had offered one sacrifice for sins for ever, sat down on the right hand of God."* (Hebrews 10:12 NIV)

In the furniture of the Tabernacle there were no seats - the priest's work was never completed. But our great high priest the Lord Jesus Christ accomplished a *"ONCE FOR ALL"* (Hebrews 10:10) offering for our sin. He would not be sitting down if there was any more work to be done. How tragic that millions of religionists are working for salvation - that is already finished and complete in Christ! Thank God for the "S" factor, or safety in Christ.

We read in Genesis 37:2 *"Joseph, being SEVENTEEN years old, was feeding the flock with his brethren."*

The first 17 years of Joseph's life were spent in the safety of his father Jacob's tents; after that till the age of 30 he was thrown into a pit, made a slave, falsely accused and languished for years in prison.

In Genesis 47:28 we read:- *"Jacob lived in Egypt SEVENTEEN years."* Jacob's life had been full of trouble, grief and adversity, but the last 17 years were the best, living in the security and sunshine of Egypt under the watchful eye of the Prime Minister, his son Joseph.

The book of Esther is the SEVENTEENTH book in our English Bible. It shows how an unseen God (because it is the only book in the Bible where His name is not mentioned) cares for His people threatened with annihilation by Haman. The books in the Hebrew Bible are arranged differently - the 17th being the book of

Jonah. It shows God's care over even a disobedient servant.

Jeremiah, who warned his people that their situation was hopeless, that they were doomed to captivity in Babylon, was given hope by the Lord. To indicate the glorious future of Israel amongst their unpromising present prospects, he was told to purchase a field in the territory of Benjamin, which he did for *"SEVENTEEN SHEKELS OF SILVER."* Copies of the purchase documents were then placed in a clay jar *"so they will last a long time. For this is what the Lord Almighty, the God of Israel says: Houses, fields and vineyards will again be bought in this land."* (Jeremiah 32:14-15 NIV)

Israel's assured repossession of their land and security therein is symbolised by *"SEVENTEEN shekels of silver"* (Jeremiah 32:9). The *"S"* factor speaks of the Sabbath Rest for Israel in the fast approaching millenial Kingdom of God. Are you beginning to taste the satisfying sweetness of the symbolism of the number SEVENTEEN?

Can a true believer ever be separated from Him? The apostle Paul was inspired by God both to ask and answer that question. In Romans 8:35 we read:- *"Who shall separate us from the love of Christ?"* (NIV)

1. *Shall tribulation*
2. *or distress*
3. *or persecution*
4. *or famine*
5. *or nakedness*
6. *or peril*
7. *or sword?"*

"As it is written, for Thy sake are we killed all the day long; we are accounted as sheep for the slaughter. Nay in ALL THESE THINGS we are more than conquerors through Him that loved us. For I am persuaded, that

8. *neither death*
9. *nor life*
10. *nor angels*
11. *nor principalities*
12. *nor powers*

13. *nor things present*
14. *nor things to come*
15. *nor height*
16. *nor depth*
17. *nor any other creature, shall be able to separate us from the love of God, which is in Christ Jesus our Lord.''*

Let us include a personal testimony at this stage. When I was writing my original book ''Times of the Signs,'' books would arrive in the mail, quite unsolicited, giving material that I needed at that exact point of time.

After the war I conducted a Bible Class on Sunday afternoons for High School boys; they were so keen that they would come to my home every Tuesday evening from 7 - 9 pm. On February 9th 1947 they presented me with a book neatly printed inside with the words - ''To Mr G.T. Curle with best wishes for the future from your Bible Class boys on the occasion of your first wedding anniversary'' appropriately signed by all the boys. The book was entitled ''The Greatest Thing in the Universe,'' The Living Word of God by LeBaron W. Kinney. It has sat on my library shelves a valued treasure for 44 years.

Recently discovering the number 17 in chronophecy I remembered Kinney's book had a chapter on the numerical value of 17 in the Bible. Turning to it I found many pages were never in the original binding right where I needed them on the number seventeen. I rang around Auckland but none of my friends had ever heard of the book - it had long been out of print. In desperation I wrote to the Publishers ''Loizeaux Brothers'' in New Jersey, U.S.A. On the 23rd August 1989 I started writing the manuscript for the ''S'' factor. The material you have read so far comes from Kinney's book but half of it was missing. That very morning photo copies of the missing pages arrived in the mail from Loizeaux Brothers. Guess when they were posted! You're dead right - the 17th August !! How very conscious I am of the Lord's leading and timing as I am writing these pages. Hallelujah! Praise His Blessed Name!

Number Seventeen - Its Meaning

In Hebrew the number 17 is made up of 7 + 10. In Bullinger's book "Number in Scripture" printed in 1894 he says the number ten "signifies the perfection of DIVINE ORDER .... completeness of order .... it implies that nothing is wanting; that the number and order are perfect; that the whole cycle is complete" (p. 243). For example the Ten Commandments contain all that is necessary, and no more than is necessary, both as to their number and order. He gives over twenty examples from Scripture.

Number seven (Sheba-Hebrew) has several meanings according to the "Theological Word Book 1980", but the important one for this study is the Hebrew verb "to swear". It is identical in the ancient text to the number seven.

In Genesis 21:23 Abimelech desires Abraham to SWEAR to deal uprightly, while Abraham in turn requires Abimelech to swear that the well of water belongs to him, Abraham. Abraham then seals the oath by giving exactly seven live lambs as a testimonial witness to Abimelech, and the well is called Beer-Sheba or well of the seven oaths.

"Oaths were serious business, especially in a nomadic society without court records and verbatim testimony. God made oaths for the benefit of the patriarchs and those who would follow them, including us who are alive today. They are a teaching method of God, a gracious instrument to help the weak of faith of every generation to believe that God will someday accomplish his promises to His people, despite discouraging external circumstances." (Theo. Word Book P. 898-901).

So combining 10 + 7 we have the symbolic meaning:-

God assuring us on oath that the complete cycle of events He has ordered will be perfectly accomplished.

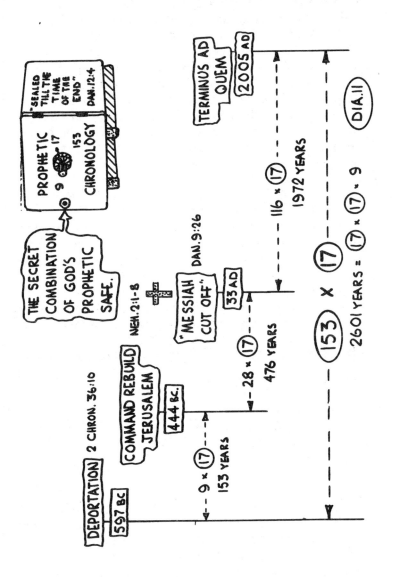

THE SECRET COMBINATION OF GOD'S PROPHETIC SAFE.

PROPHETIC CHRONOLOGY
9 17 153

"SEALED TILL THE TIME OF THE END" DAN.12:4

DEPORTATION 2 CHRON. 36:16
597 B.C.

COMMAND REBUILD JERUSALEM NEH.2:1-8
444 B.C.

"MESSIAH CUT OFF" DAN.9:26
33 A.D.

TERMINUS AD QUEM
2005 AD

9 × 17 153 YEARS

28 × 17 476 YEARS

116 × 17 1972 YEARS

153 × 17
2601 YEARS = 17 × 17 × 9

DIA.11

Seventeen And Chronophecy

The 69 Weeks of Daniel (Dia. No. 11)

From the command to rebuild Jerusalem (Nehemiah 2:1-8) 444 B.C. to Messiah being cut off in 33 A.D. is 476 solar years, which is exactly 28 x 17 years or 4 x 7 x 17. From 444 B.C. to our terminal year 2005 A.D. is 2448 years or 12 x 12 x 17. Twelve speaks of God's administrative power, and when it is multiplied by itself we see an intensified form of the meaning of twelve. This prophecy in Daniel 9 is the vertebrate of chronological prophecy and it is stamped throughout with the wondrous number SEVENTEEN:-

GOD ASSURING US ON OATH THAT THE COMPLETE CYCLE OF EVENTS HE HAS ORDERED WILL BE PERFECTLY ACCOMPLISHED.

Sixty nine of these seven year cycles have been fulfilled exactly to the appointed predicted time - giving us complete confidence that the final seven years (the 70th week) will also run perfectly to its prophetic timetable. These seventy seven year cycles are linked to an even longer time span as we shall now see as we travel further on this exciting voyage of discovery.

The Deportation 597 B.C. (Dia. No. 11)

The main bulk of Jerusalem's inhabitants were deported to Babylon in 597 B.C. (2 Kings 24:10-15, 2 Chronicles 36:10). "Nebuchadnezzar besieged Jerusalem and captured the city on Saturday 16th March 597 B.C." (Mysterious Number Hebrew Kings p. 186 3rd Edition).

I measured the time span from 597 B.C. to 444 B.C., the terminus a quo for the 70 weeks of Daniel. It came to one hundred and fifty three years! That is 9 x 17 = 153! Nine, the number of finality, the conclusion of a matter multiplied with the sweetness of seventeen coming to 153. What importance has the number 153?

The 153 Fishes (John 21:11)

153 is the exact number of fish in the net Peter dragged ashore.

This exact number of fish has tantalised

commentators for almost nineteen centuries. William Barclay says :- "In the fourth Gospel everything is meaningful, and it is hardly possible that John gives the definite number one hundred and fifty three for the number of fishes without meaning something by it." Gospel of John p. 328.

Many of the suggestions put forward are found in "Number in Scripture" by Bullinger.

"We might give yet another contribution to these various modes as the result of our investigations in numbers, and say that 153 = 9 x 17, and see in this number all judgment (9) exhausted for the people of God (17) in the persons of their surety .... the one lesson that remains is true, namely, that the whole number of the redeemed are saved by the power of the Triune God. We may condense all this by calling 153 simply :- THE NUMBER OF THE SONS OF GOD. The expression "Sons of God" occurs seven times, and the value of the Hebrew letters is exactly 153!" (Number in Scripture pgs. 274-275)

The net that was "not broken" represents all the redeemed - lets look at it first as a Jewish net, then as the Church net.

The Jewish Net

What I am about to show you represents truly one of the highlights of my trailblazing into the vast forest of chronophecy. The desert of dates truly blossomed with chronoprophetic roses. Praise God, the one who has *"NUMBERED the very hairs of our head"* (Matthew 10:30) has NUMBERED and ORDERED the very years of Israel's DISPERSION (Diaspora) - (Dia. 11). From the captivity in 597 B.C. to the terminal year of 2005 A.D. is exactly 2601 years which is precisely 153 x 17!! or 17 x 17 x 9!!

These numbers represent the fullest expression possible of that wondrous number 17:-

GOD ASSURING US ON OATH THAT THE COMPLETE CYCLE OF EVENTS HE HAS ORDERED WILL BE PERFECTLY ACCOMPLISHED.

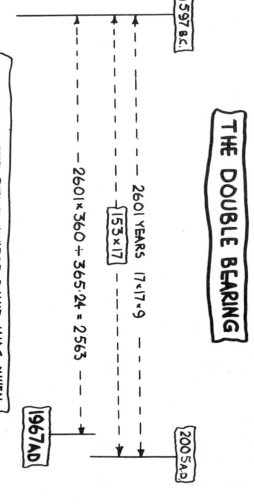

THE DOUBLE BEARING

597 B.C.

2601 YEARS 17×17×9

153×17

2601×360÷365·24 = 2563

1967 AD

2005 A.D.

"WE ARE AT THE STAGE WHERE DAVID WAS WHEN HE LIBERATED JERUSALEM. FROM THAT TIME UNTIL THE CONSTRUCTION OF THE TEMPLE BY SOLOMON, ONLY **ONE GENERATION** PASSES, SO WILL IT BE WITH US." [ISRAEL ELDAD]

DIA.12

Now to put the icing on the cake; remember how past bearings when changed from solar years and counted as prophetic years always yielded a year of tremendous prophetic significance in Israel's history, so changing 2601 solar years and calling them 2601 prophetic years they become 2601 x 360 ÷ 365.24 = 2563 years. Measuring 2563 years from 597 B.C. we come into 1967 A.D.!! The year of the six day war and the capture of the Temple Mount (Dia. 12) was one of the most prophetic years for centuries!!

Having iced the cake with this double bearing let us now place some decoration on the icing. It is quite amazing how words that will have a special significance in the end time are mentioned exactly 17 times in the New Testament. Take the word 'Fulness' for example :-
"until the FULNESS of the Gentiles be come in" (Romans 11:25).
"dispensation of the FULNESS of times" (Ephesians 1:10).
The word *"Until"*:-
"grow together UNTIL the harvest" (Matthew 13:30).
"UNTIL the appearing of our Lord Jesus Christ" (1 Timothy 6:14).
"rejoicing of the hope firm UNTIL the end" (Hebrews 3:6).
"Steadfast UNTIL the end" (Hebrews 3:14).
The word *"Ready"*:-
"The wedding is READY" (Matthew 22:8).
"be ye also READY" (Matthew 24:44).
The word *"JUDGE"*:-
"the JUDGE standeth before the door" (James 5:9).
"the JUDGE of the quick and the dead" (Acts 10:42).

There are exactly 17 historical books (Genesis to Esther) and 17 prophetic books (Isaiah to Malachi). What God has established in history is our guarantee of what He will accomplish in the future. For example in His prophetic sermon (Matthew 24-25, Mark 13 and Luke 21) our Lord gave a short range prophecy, the destruction of the Temple, fall of Jerusalem and Diaspora, as well as a long range prophecy of end time events that will be fulfilled in the same literal manner as the A.D. 70 events.

If we measure 153 x 17 years from 605 B.C. (Nebuchadnezzar's first year) we come exactly to 1997 A.D.

1000 Prophetic Years (Dia. 13)

Do you remember in the Times of the Millenia (Chap. 2 'Times of the Signs') we learnt that one thousand prophetic years is equivalent to nine hundred and eighty six solar years. 1000 x 360 ÷ 365.2421 = 986 to nearest round year. Plotting from 33 A.D. "one day" of 986 years we come to 1019 A.D., and "two days" to 2005 A.D. (p.34) Now 986 is 58 x 17! (p.27-35). If we measure Methuselah's life span (969 yrs) from 1019 A.D. (p.139) we come to 1988 A.D. i.e. 57 x 17 one short, add one more 17 and we come to 2005 A.D.

"Noah's name in Hebrew is made up of the number 8 + 50 = 58! The word "grace" is the word "Noah" spelt backwards 50 + 8 and equals 58. The number 58 speaks of grace in many passages." (Le Baron Kinney)

The word "Hallelujah" in the Greek has the value of 580 or 10 x 58 the perfect ordering (10) of God's grace (58) in redemptive history. Each one of the time spans of 986 years in bearing No. 1 thus has "Hallelujah" embedded in it, or "Praise Ye The Lord."

"In Revelation 19:1-6 the Hallelujah chorus is sung in Heaven! Four times the two words, dropped out of the vocabulary of the angels into the various tongues of men, are lifted high: "Hallelujah! Amen!" Those two words seem to be the same in all the languages of men. They are the praise words of heavenly hosts, loaned to men to help them voice their worship of the Lord. They are part of a universal tongue.

Two men once met aboard an ocean liner, the one was white the other black. They had never met before; both were Christians; both felt out of place among the

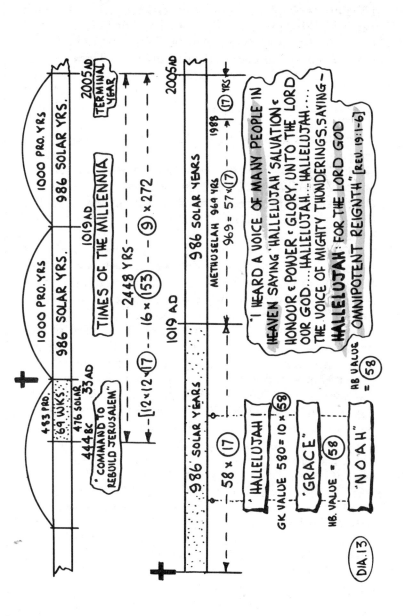

"I HEARD A VOICE OF MANY PEOPLE IN HEAVEN SAYING 'HALLELUJAH' SALVATION & HONOUR & POWER & GLORY, UNTO THE LORD OUR GOD....HALLELUJAH...HALLELUJAH..... THE VOICE OF MIGHTY THUNDERINGS, SAYING—

HALLELUJAH: FOR THE LORD GOD OMNIPOTENT REIGNTH" [REV. 19:1-6]

DIA. 13

frivolous and pleasure seeking crowds on deck. Each carried a Bible in his hand. They met, shook hands, and tried to exchange a few words of Christian greeting, but the barrier of language stood between. Then one of them had an idea. "Hallelujah!" he said, to which the other replied, "Amen!" They had found a common tongue of praise." (Exploring Revelation John Philips p.239).

The last seventeen years to the end started ticking over in 1988 - soon there are to be two great events - a wedding in Heaven (Revelation 19:7-10) and war on earth (Revelation 19:11-21). The Church, the world and Israel come to the consummation of their ways. Oh the joy, the wonder, the glory that is now so close at hand for the Christian.

"The book of Revelation so full of sorrow, strife and tears, is also a book filled with song! (Revelation 14:2-3). Bring the Lamb into the picture, and immediately there is song! The Lord has an amazing ability to make His people happy. One of the wonders of the God of the Bible is that He is a HAPPY God! The gods of the pagans are fierce, wicked and cruel, delighting in the tears and tremblings of men and feasting on human fear. But our God is a happy God. He picks us up from the horrible pit, plants our feet upon the rock, and puts a new song into our mouth. One of the greatest lessons we can learn in life is simply there can be no real happiness apart from true holiness. God is altogether holy; therefore He is altogether happy. When we are filled with the Spirit, we sing! (Psalm 40:2-3; Ephesians 5:18-19). This exalted company of God's people is also an exultant company. They fill the courts of heaven with their song until the very hills thunder back the sound." (Exploring Revelation p. 187 John Phillips)

58, 17, 58, 17 Hallelujah! Amen! Hallelujah! Amen!
"Hallelujah! For our Lord God Almighty reigns"
(Revelation 19:6)

Chapter Five

The Sound Of Music (Dia. 24)
(ISA. 30:32 NIV)

Incredible as it may seem there is a harmonic relationship between the notes of the musical scale and the chronological history of Israel. For example:-

"By international agreement reached in 1955 the
frequency of the note A to which the orchestra is
traditionally tuned in 440HZ"
(McGraw Hill Science and Technology Vo. 8. p.827)

Musical frequencies are shown in HERTZ, a term which simply means "cycles per second" when instruments are to be played in unison they must be tuned to the same pitch - now normally A = 440HZ.

Likewise Israel's history can be traced in a similar fashion as we will demonstrate later, but just to whet your appetite, from the year when Isaac (B.C. 1846) inherited until the children of Israel entered the promised land in B.C. 1406 is exactly 440 years!

Sound And Music (Dia. 14)

"Sound is the impression produced on the ear by vibrations of air. The pitch of the musical note is higher or lower accordingly as these vibrations become faster or slower. When they are too slow or not sufficiently regular and continuous to make a musical sound we call it noise.

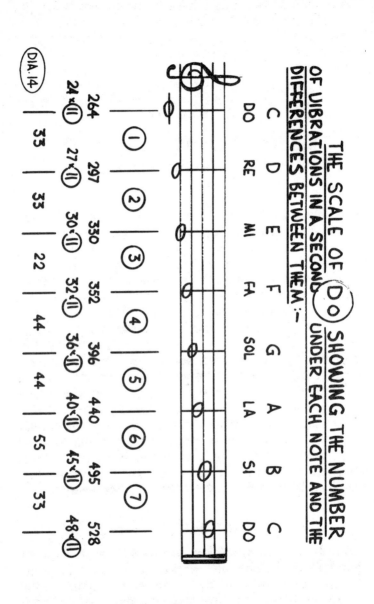

THE SCALE OF DO SHOWING THE NUMBER
OF VIBRATIONS IN A SECOND UNDER EACH NOTE AND THE
DIFFERENCES BETWEEN THEM :-

	C	D	E	F	G	A	B	C
	DO	RE	MI	FA	SOL	LA	SI	DO
	①	②	③	④	⑤	⑥	⑦	
	264	297	330	352	396	440	495	528
	24×⑪	27×⑪	30×⑪	32×⑪	36×⑪	40×⑪	45×⑪	48×⑪
	33	33	22	44	44	55	33	

DIA. 14

Experiments have long been completed which fix the number of vibrations for each musical note; by which of course we may calculate the difference between the number of vibrations between each note.

These were finally settled at Stuttgart in 1834. They were adopted by the Paris conservatoire in 1859, but it was not till 1869 that they were adopted in England by the Society of Arts. Dia. 14 is the scale of 'do' showing the number of vibrations in a second under each note and the differences between them.

In the upper row of figures, those immediately under each note are the number of vibrations proceeding such note. The figures in brackets between these numbers show the difference between these vibrations. The figures in the lower line are merely the factors of the respective numbers. On examining the above it will be seen at once that the number ELEVEN is stamped up on music; and we may say SEVEN also, for there are seven notes of the scale (The eighth being the repetition of the first). The number of vibrations between each note is also a multiple of ELEVEN."

(Number in Scripture Bullinger p.15/16). "Sunspots occur in regular eleven year cycles". You may be interested to know how I came to link the above facts of music, which I had known from my early teens, with the chronological history of Israel which I have discovered in my late sixties! I was down at Whitianga (home of the Mercury Bay Yacht Club of America's Cup Fame), conducting a water-colour painting workshop with the local Art Society. In my limited spare time I was reading two books on the numerical structure of scripture:-

1. The Greatest Thing in the Universe
   by Le Baron W. Kiney (1939)
2. The Numerical Structure of Scripture
   by F.W. Grant (1887)

Whitianga is on the Coromandel Peninsula, full of history of earlier gold rushes - so these words of F.W. Grant really struck home. After showing some of the wonders of Bible numerics he says:-

"Is this the way then, in which scripture is written? or are these merely exceptional instances? Beloved friends, when a man prospecting for ore comes upon a seam of metal on the surface of a rock, he does not readily believe that that which comes just before his eyes is all that is to be found there. And geologists have remarked upon the special providential care that has tilted up and broken across the strata of the earth as it were, just to make known to man the stores deeply packed away. Had they lain just as, ages ago, they were deposited, we might forever have been ignorant of the wealth lying in the bowels of the earth for us. And has not God in these scriptures just exposed to us, as it were, the heads of precious veins which lie deeper? Would he not have us follow them out, and see to what they lead?.... Alas! instead of following them out, we have refused to recognise in this strange human guise the God who comes to meet us thus, and once more dropped out of our hands a clue that would have led us on to a wealth of blessing. (p.16)

No wonder the Psalmist could say -

"The law from your mouth is more precious to me than thousands of pieces of silver and gold." (Psalm 119:72 NIV)

"I love your commands more than gold, more than pure gold." (Psalm 119:127 NIV)

"The ordinances of the Lord are sure, and altogether righteous. They are more precious than gold, than much pure gold." (Psalm 19:9-10)

And then I read in Kinney's book -

"The number system of God is stamped on all His works. There are multiples of eleven vibrations that come between each note. The same God who created all things stamped this number upon music and song in scripture. We find the number 'eleven' connected with song, music, harmony and feasting everywhere in the word of God."

The first song in the word of God is the song of Moses, and the last song is the "song of the Lamb." There are many patterns of eleven connected with the "Song of Moses" .... even the name "Moses" is wrought into a design of elevens. The name "Moses" occurs just 7 x 11 x 11 or 847 times in the Bible! The last occurence of the name "Moses" is in the book of Revelation, where it is mentioned only once. This completes the wonderful pattern. None of the other writers could possibly have known they were weaving a part of such a design .... (Dia. 15)

The Hebrew word "feast" chag, has the value of eleven." (Dia. 16)

There are twenty-three pages in his book showing the wonderful numerics of "eleven" in the Word of God, but I will not weary you with all the marvellous details.

Saturday, the last day of the painting workshop was very busy, we completed three paintings! They told me most instructors only do one a day. My body clock is more that of a fowl than an owl. It's my practice to retire at 9.30 p.m. and rise at 4 a.m. for study. So by 9.35 p.m. on this particular Saturday night I was in a deep sleep. Suddenly I was unusually awake just after 10 p.m. The number "eleven" was whirling around in my mind. Having switched on the light I reached out for my constant travelling companion, my 'Sharp' pocket calculator.

Calculating The 'Eleven Year' Cycles

Setting the figure at B.C. 1846 when Isaac became the heir I ran through time to A.D. 2005 in eleven year spans - jotting on a piece of paper any key important dates connected with Israel. To my surprise there were only eight, including Isaac, giving us only SEVEN time spans in multiples of "ELEVEN" just as there are on a musical scale, and coinciding exactly with A.D. 2005! Here are the dates I jotted down:-

B.C. 1846, 1406, 966, 515, 20

A.D. 69, 1917, 2005

It seemed God was playing a tune with Israel's history - there was certainly order, harmony, a feasting in these apparent random dates in history. There was little sleep that night, I was excited with awesome

73

THE SONG OF MOSES

"I WILL SING TO THE LORD, FOR HE IS HIGHLY EXALTED.
THE HORSE AND HIS RIDER HE HAS HURLED INTO THE SEA.
THE LORD IS MY STRENGTH AND MY SONG;
HE HAS BECOME MY SALVATION,
HE IS MY GOD AND I WILL PRAISE HIM." [EX.15:1-2]

FIRST & LAST SONG IN THE BIBLE "SONG OF MOSES" [EX.15, REV.15:3]

THE WORD "MOSES" OCCURS 847 TIMES IN THE BIBLE = 77 × (11)

THE SONG IS INTRODUCED BY THE WORDS:- "THEN SANG MOSES, AND
THE CHILDREN OF ISRAEL THIS SONG UNTO THE LORD, AND SPAKE SAYING,"-
THIS INTRODUCTION IS EXPRESSED IN HEBREW WITH ELEVEN WORDS, & FOUR
TIMES ELEVEN, OR 44 LETTERS. THE WORDS "THEN SANG"
HAVE THE VALUE OF 48 ×11 OR 4×12 ×11. TWELVE SPEAKS OF
GOD RULING, REIGNING, TRIUMPHING. THE ENEMY HAD BEEN
OVERCOME IN THE RED SEA; GOD HAD TRIUMPHED -"THEN
SANG MOSES"   Le BARON W. KINNEY.

THERE WAS NO SINGING IN EGYPT.

(DIA.15)

74

"FEAST" = ג + ח   CHAG

GIMEL CHETH
3 + 8 = (11)

"THE NUMBER ELEVEN SPEAKS OF THE MUSIC & HARMONY THAT GOES WITH FEASTING." KINNEY

"THE VERB IS USED SPECIFICALLY FOR THE CELEBRATION OF THE OF THE THREE MAIN PILGRIM-FEASTS :-

① THE PASSOVER TOGETHER WITH THE FEAST OF UNLEAVENED BREAD.

② THE FEAST OF WEEKS OR HARVEST OF FIRSTFRUITS.

③ THE FEAST OF BOOTHS (TABERNACLES) OR FEAST OF INGATHERING " [THEO. WORDBOOK O.T.]

"LET MY PEOPLE GO THAT THEY MAY HOLD A FEAST UNTO ME IN THE WILDERNESS" [EX. 4:31, 5:1]

(DIA. 16)

75

wonder at God's hand in history. If someone had offered me all the gold that has ever been mined in those Coromandel ranges it would be but dross compared to the pure gold to which the Holy Spirit had led me in the Word of God and history.

"The ordinances of the Lord are sure, and altogether righteous. They are more precious than gold, than much pure gold." (Psalm 19:9-10 NIV)

On the Sunday morning I preached in the local Baptist church on the marvellous number 17 (see 'S' factor) as advertised - but it was hard to refrain from going on to explain the number 11 in numerics and history.

The Musical Scale Of History (Dia. 17)

Note DO. Isaac inherits B.C. 1846

"The child grew and was weaned, and on the day that Isaac was weaned Abraham held a great feast." (Genesis 21:8 NIV)

Time started ticking for Israel from that moment. God blessed, when Abraham broke off his relationship completely with Hagar. Paul wrote to the churches in Galatia, *"You foolish Galatians! WHO has bewitched you?"* (Galatians 3:1) "WHO" implies a person in the life. You will never know God's full blessings while there is a beautiful Hagar or a strong Ishmael in your tent. F.B. Meyer says - "In what way the presence of Hagar and Ishmael hindered the development of Abraham's noblest life of faith, we cannot entirely understand. Did his heart still cling to the girl who had given him his firstborn son? Was there any secret satisfaction in the arrangement, which at least achieved one cherished purpose, though it had been unblessed by God? Was there any fear that if summoned to surrender Isaac, he would find it easier to do so, because at any moment, he could fall back on Ishmael, as both son and heir? We cannot read all that was in Abraham's mind; but surely some such thoughts are suggested by the expressions which to this hour record the history of the anguish of this torn and lonely heart, as one darling idol after

76

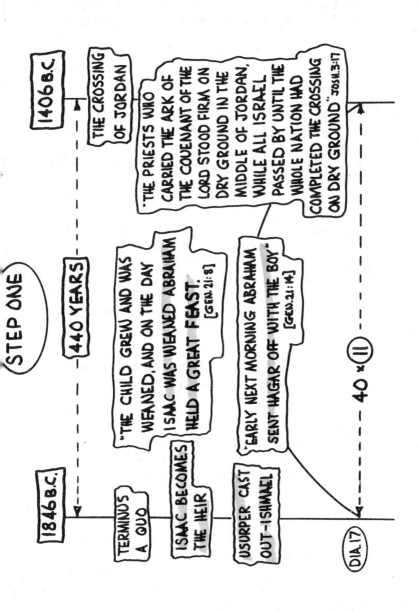

STEP ONE

1406 B.C.

THE CROSSING OF JORDAN

"THE PRIESTS WHO CARRIED THE ARK OF THE COVENANT OF THE LORD STOOD FIRM ON DRY GROUND IN THE MIDDLE OF JORDAN, WHILE ALL ISRAEL PASSED BY UNTIL THE WHOLE NATION HAD COMPLETED THE CROSSING ON DRY GROUND" JOSH. 3:17

440 YEARS

"THE CHILD GREW AND WAS WEANED, AND ON THE DAY ISAAC WAS WEANED ABRAHAM HELD A GREAT FEAST." [GEN. 21:8]

"EARLY NEXT MORNING ABRAHAM SENT HAGAR OFF WITH THE BOY" [GEN. 21:14]

1846 B.C.

TERMINUS A QUO

ISAAC BECOMES THE HEIR

USURPER CAST OUT—ISHMAEL

40 × 11

DIA. 17

77

another was rent away, that he himself might be cast naked and helpless on the omnipotence of the Eternal God "The thing was very grievous in Abraham's sight" (v.11)....

The remaining history is briefly told. With many a pang - as the vine which bleeds copiously when the pruning knife is doing its work - Abraham sent Hagar and her child forth from his home, bidding them a last sad farewell. In the dim twilight they fared forth, before the camp was awakened. The strong man must have suffered keenly as he put the bread into her hand, and with his own fingers bound the bottle of water on her shoulder, and kissed Ishmael once more and yet he must not let Sarah guess how much he felt it. How many passages in our lives are known only to God....

That which seems to break our hearts at the moment, turns out in after years to have been of God." (O.T. Men of Faith p. 81/86). Man of God, whatever it takes drive Hagar from your tent - "A wise monkey never monkeys with another monkey's monkey." "The man who thinks he can cheat a moral God in a moral universe, is a moral imbecile."

Note Re: Entrance Into Canaan B.C. 1406 (Joshua 3)

All orchestras of the world tune up their instruments to concert pitch 440HZ. Likewise the master musician tunes up Israel's history with an initial time span of 440 years! What rejoicing, what feasting, we can be sure, when they crossed Jordan and placed their feet for the first time on their Promised Land.

But there can be no blessings without battles. God blessed Abraham in 1846 through a bleeding heart - now he cannot bless the nation without blood. *"At the time the Lord said to Joshua, make flint knives and circumcise the Israelites .... and after the whole nation had been circumcised, they remained where they were in camp until they were healed."* (Joshua 5:2,8)

"The New Testament analogy is world conformity,

78

the failure openly to take a believer's place with Christ in death and resurrection. (Romans 6:2-11 and Galatians 6:14-16). Spiritually, circumcision is putting to death the deeds of the body through the Spirit (Romans 8:13, Galatians 5:16-17, Colossians 2:11-12, 3:5-10) (New Scofield Bible footnote Joshua 5:2)

How deeply painful for mature men to be circumcised at that time, with no local anaesthetic, or stainless steel surgical knives. But there could be no victories in Canaan, no conquests, no blessings until the knife had been applied.

Note. B.C. 966 Solomon's Temple Started (Dia. 18)

Another 440 years (40 x11) from B.C. 1406 comes to B.C. 966.

"In the four hundred and eightieth year after the Israelites had come out of Egypt, in the fourth year of Solomon's reign over Israel, in the month of Ziv, the second month he began to build the Temple of the Lord." (1 Kings 6:1)

Just as note A is 440 cycles per second, and is used to tune instruments into unison, so God uses the span of 440 years i.e. 40 x 11 not once but twice in launching the musical chronology of Israel. What rejoicing, what feasting this historic occasion would have been - after 480 years worshipping Jehovah in a temporary, portable structure of animal skins to actually have a permanent temple in stone!

Using this 440 year time span, not once, but twice emphasises God's control of history - do you recognise it?

"For God speaketh once, yea twice, yet man perceiveth it not." (Job 33:14)

"God hath spoken once; twice have I heard this; that power belongs unto God." (Psalm 66:11)

Is your heart fearful of all the sudden, crashing changes that are taking place in world events? - or is your heart singing, at peace, tranquil as our God with measured cycles brings history to a glorious climax?

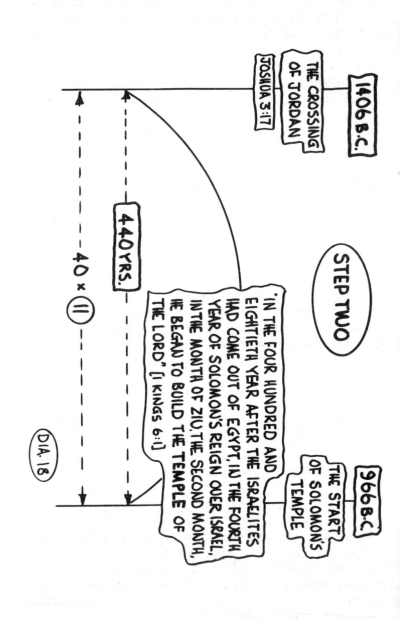

THE CROSSING OF JORDAN

JOSHUA 3:17

1406 B.C.

440 YRS.

40 × ⑪

STEP TWO

"IN THE FOUR HUNDRED AND EIGHTIETH YEAR AFTER THE ISRAELITES HAD COME OUT OF EGYPT, IN THE FOURTH YEAR OF SOLOMON'S REIGN OVER ISRAEL, IN THE MONTH OF ZIV, THE SECOND MONTH, HE BEGAN TO BUILD THE TEMPLE OF THE LORD." [1 KINGS 6:1]

DIA. 18

THE START OF SOLOMON'S TEMPLE

966 B.C.

"Then the sovereignty, power and greatness of the kingdoms under the whole heaven will be handed over to the saints, the people of the Most High. His Kingdom will be an everlasting Kingdom, and all rulers will worship and obey Him." (Daniel 7:27)

Note. B.C. 515 Second Temple Dedicated (Dia. 19)

41 eleven year cycles from B.C. 966 comes to the year B.C. 515 - a time span of 451 years.

"And this temple was completed on the third day of the month Adar; it was the sixth year of the reign of King Darius ("the sixth year of Darius was B.C. 516-515" Speaker's commentary) *and the sons of Israel, the priests, the Levites, and the rest of the exiles, celebrated the dedication of this house of God with joy."* (Ezra 6:15-16 NIV)

After seventy years captivity in idolatrous Babylon, built on alluvial soil, what a joyous experience for these exiles to ascend 2,500 feet above sea level, and there build their second temple on solid cretaceous rock.

"And the sons of Israel who returned from exile and all those who had separated themselves from the IMPURITY of the nations of the land to join them, to SEEK the Lord God of Israel, ate the Passover, and they observed the FEAST of Unleavened Bread seven days with JOY, for the Lord had caused them to REJOICE." (Ezra 6:22-22 NASB)

Separation from impurity leads to joy and rejoicing.

"Who may ascend the hill of the Lord?
Who may stand in His holy place?
He who has clean hands and a pure heart.
Who does not lift up his soul to an idol or swear
by what is false.
He will receive blessing from the Lord and
vindication from God his saviour." (Psalm 24:3-5 NASB)

Is your spiritual vitality being sapped by world conformity and the "impurity of the nations"?

You would be horrified if your local city council made a pipe connection from the untreated sewage ponds to your own living room, then gushed the contents over

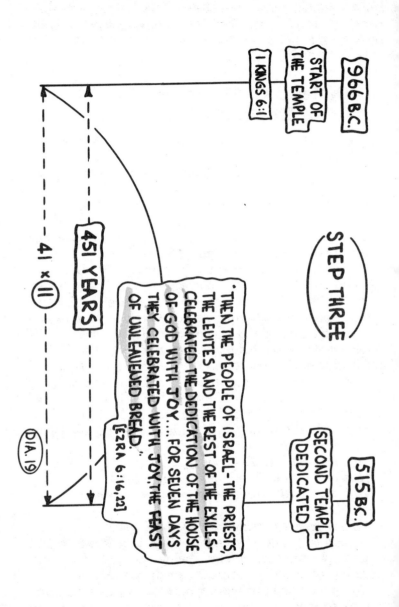

STEP THREE

966 B.C.

START OF
THE TEMPLE

1 KINGS 6:1

451 YEARS

41 × 11

DIA.19

"THEN THE PEOPLE OF ISRAEL - THE PRIESTS,
THE LEVITES AND THE REST OF THE EXILES -
CELEBRATED THE DEDICATION OF THE HOUSE
OF GOD WITH JOY.... FOR SEVEN DAYS
THEY CELEBRATED WITH JOY, THE FEAST
OF UNLEAVENED BREAD."

[EZRA 6:16, 22]

515 B.C.

SECOND TEMPLE
DEDICATED

your carpet. More and more, our TV sets are becoming sewage pipes into our lounge, turning us into spiritual pygmies. If one spends four hours each evening watching TV then in one week they have spent 28 hours - more than a whole day a week! In one year, two months would be spent waste watching!

4 hours x 7 = 28 hours per week
28 x 52 = 1456 hours per annum
1456 divided by 24 = 60.666 days per annum!

Are you voluntarily stamping this number of the beast into your subconscious mind? Can you justify 60.666 days or two months each year glued to mind-destroying, banal, hypnotic trivia?

In the light of the nearness of our Lord's return, how do we respond to these verses?

"Making the MOST OF YOUR TIME, because the days are EVIL" (Ephesians 5:16 NASB)

"Walking in wisdom toward those who are outside REDEEMING THE TIME." (Colossians 4:5 NKJV)

"I will walk within my house in the integrity of my heart. I will set no worthless thing before my eyes; .... it shall not fasten its grip on me." (Psalm 101:2-3 N.A.S.B.)

Note B.C. 20 The Start Of Herod's Temple (Dia. 20)

Another cycle of 405 years (45 x 11) brings us to the year B.C. 20 - the year Herod superseded Zerubbabel's temple by building a lavish magnificent temple for the Jews.

In an endeavour to win popularity with the Jews King Herod declared that Zerubbabel's Temple was not worthy of their past. There must be another as glorious as craftsmanship and wealth could meet. This temple exceeded Solomon's in magnificence and architectural beauty. In the eighteenth year of his reign 20 B.C., Herod began the reconstruction of the Temple. He removed one part after another of Zerubbabel's sacred buildings, only to man a more magnificent fane. He had some of the priests taught stone cutting and carpentering that the Holy House might be built by them. Thousands of highly skilled workmen were employed, and the noble edifice was adorned with gold, silver and the finest marble from Greece.

Note A.D. 69 Jerusalem Beseiged (Dia. 21)

88 years on from 20 B.C. brings us to A.D. 69 which is eight spans of 11 years. How could the siege of Jerusalem be a cause for music, praise and rejoicing, when in A.D. 70 over a million Jews lost their lives through fire, carnage, rape and massacre in a Warsaw Ghetto type disaster?

This appalling tragedy occurred because the Jewish nation rejected their Messiah - the Lord Jesus Christ *"He came unto His Own, and His own received Him not"* (John 1:11)

But at that time, living in the city were those who had received Him as Saviour - the early church. Jesus gave them clear instructions *"When you see Jerusalem surrounded by armies, then recognise that her desolation is near."* (Luke 21:20 NKJV)

In A.D. 69 the Christians escaped from the city to Pella in Trans-Jordan. What praise and worship must have ascended from those who were delivered from the Roman siege and destruction of Jerusalem, a foretaste of the redeemed church universally delivered world-wide before the Tribulation.

Note A.D. 1917 British Capture Jerusalem (Dia. 22)

After a long span of eleven year cycles from A.D. 69 we come again to another prophetic year A.D. 1917, 1848 years (168 x 11). What a year of rejoicing and praise! The Turks had held Jerusalem for exactly 400 years.

"At dawn on Dec. 8th 1917, General Allenby attacked Jerusalem (although not a single shell fell on Jerusalem

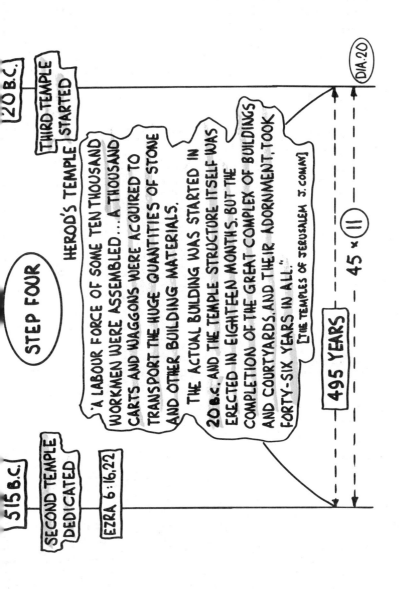

STEP FOUR

520 B.C. THIRD TEMPLE STARTED

515 B.C. SECOND TEMPLE DEDICATED

EZRA 6:16,22

HEROD'S TEMPLE

"A LABOUR FORCE OF SOME TEN THOUSAND WORKMEN WERE ASSEMBLED... A THOUSAND CARTS AND WAGGONS WERE ACQUIRED TO TRANSPORT THE HUGE QUANTITIES OF STONE AND OTHER BUILDING MATERIALS.

THE ACTUAL BUILDING WAS STARTED IN 20 B.C. AND THE TEMPLE STRUCTURE ITSELF WAS ERECTED IN EIGHTEEN MONTHS. BUT THE COMPLETION OF THE GREAT COMPLEX OF BUILDINGS AND COURTYARDS, AND THEIR ADORNMENT, TOOK FORTY-SIX YEARS IN ALL."

[THE TEMPLES OF JERUSALEM J. COMAY]

495 YEARS

45 × 11

DIA. 20

85

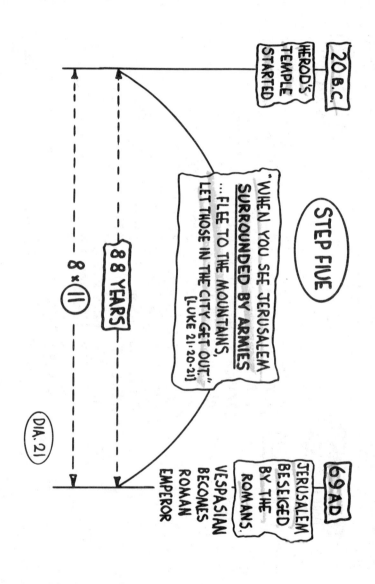

STEP FIVE

20 B.C. — HEROD'S TEMPLE STARTED

"WHEN YOU SEE JERUSALEM SURROUNDED BY ARMIES ...FLEE TO THE MOUNTAINS, LET THOSE IN THE CITY GET OUT." [LUKE 21:20-21]

8 × 11

88 YEARS

DIA. 21

69 AD — JERUSALEM BESEIGED BY THE ROMANS. VESPASIAN BECOMES ROMAN EMPEROR

86

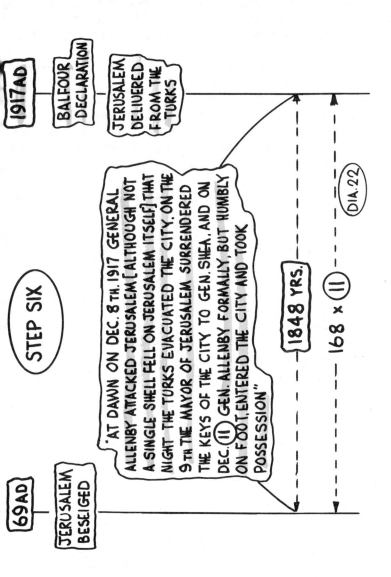

STEP SIX

1917 AD

BALFOUR DECLARATION

JERUSALEM DELIVERED FROM THE TURKS

"AT DAWN ON DEC. 8TH, 1917 GENERAL ALLENBY ATTACKED JERUSALEM [ALTHOUGH NOT A SINGLE SHELL FELL ON JERUSALEM ITSELF] THAT NIGHT—THE TURKS EVACUATED THE CITY. ON THE 9TH THE MAYOR OF JERUSALEM SURRENDERED THE KEYS OF THE CITY TO GEN. SHEA. AND ON DEC. 11 GEN. ALLENBY FORMALLY, BUT HUMBLY ON FOOT, ENTERED THE CITY AND TOOK POSSESSION."

69 AD

JERUSALEM BESEIGED

1848 YRS.

168 × 11

DIA. 22

87

itself). That night the Turks evacuated the city. On the 9th, the Mayor of Jerusalem surrendered the keys of the city to General Shea, and on Dec. 11th, General Allenby formally but humbly on foot, entered the city and took possession."

Christians around the world, who knew the prophetic scriptures were ecstatic with delight. The 'Second Advent Testimony League' was formed in England. Grattan Guiness in 'Light for the last Days' in 1886, had singled out 1917 A.D. as an important prophetic date. He says "The year 1917 is consequently doubly indicated as a final crisis date." (p.343)

Note A.D. 2005 End Of Gentile World Domination (Dia. 23)

To complete our musical scale we come to another eight eleven year cycles to 2005 A.D.! Note 1948 and 1967 do not coincide with this eleven year pattern. They were years of bloodshed. There are only seven spans of eleven year cycles from Isaac to 2005 A.D. that vitally connect with Israel's prophetic history! Just as there are only seven spans of (eleven cycles per second) multiples of vibrations in the musical scale.

What rejoicing in Heaven and in Earth when Antichrist, Satan and all enemies of the Lord are dethroned. Just as we have seen tyrants toppled in Eastern Europe who lived in palaces and extravagant luxury whilst their subjects were living in poverty. In that day we will sing as Israel sang after their deliverance out of Egypt:-

"I will sing to the Lord, for He is highly exalted; the horse and the rider He has hurled into the sea .... Thou wilt bring them and plant them in the mountain of thine inheritance, the place, O Lord, which Thou hast made for Thy dwelling, Thy sanctuary, O lord, which Thy hands have established. The Lord shall reign forever and ever. (Exodus 15:17-18)

How the sound of singing and music will fill Heaven forever.

"I saw in heaven another great and marvellous sign, seven

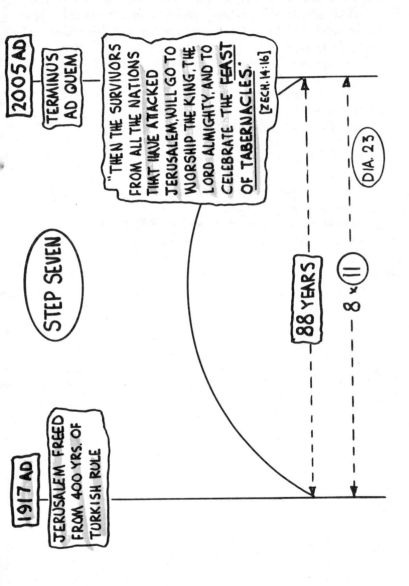

STEP SEVEN

1917 AD

JERUSALEM FREED FROM 400 YRS. OF TURKISH RULE

2005 AD

TERMINUS AD QUEM

"THEN THE SURVIVORS FROM ALL THE NATIONS THAT HAVE ATTACKED JERUSALEM WILL GO TO WORSHIP THE KING, THE LORD ALMIGHTY, AND TO CELEBRATE THE FEAST OF TABERNACLES." [ZECH. 14:16]

88 YEARS

8 × 11

DIA. 23

89

angels with the seven last plagues - last, because with them
God's wrath is completed. And I saw what looked like a sea
of glass mixed with fire and, standing beside the sea, those
who had been victorious over the beast, and his image and
over the number of his name. They held harps given them by
God, and sang the song of Moses the servant of God, and the
song of the Lamb:

Great and marvellous are your deeds,
Lord God Almighty.
Just and true are your ways,
King of the Ages.
Who will not fear you,
O Lord,
And bring glory to your name?
For you alone are Holy.
All nations will come and worship before you,
for your righteous acts have been revealed.''

(Revelation 15: 1-4 NIV)

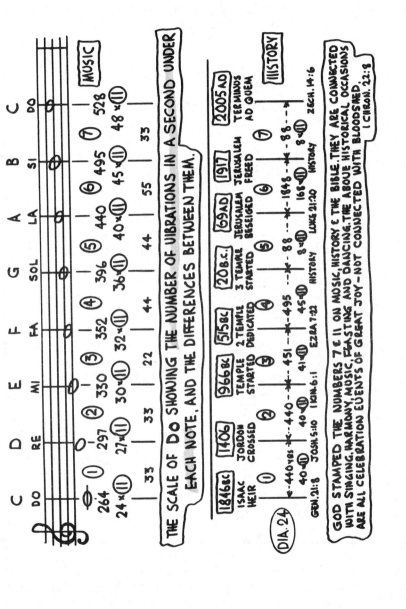

MUSIC

C	D	E	F	G	A	B	C
DO	RE	MI	FA	SOL	LA	SI	DO
①	②	③	④	⑤	⑥	⑦	
264	297	330	352	396	440	495	528
24×⑪	27×⑪	30×⑪	32×⑪	36×⑪	40×⑪	45×⑪	48×⑪
33	33	22	44	44	55	33	

THE SCALE OF **DO** SHOWING THE NUMBER OF VIBRATIONS IN A SECOND UNDER EACH NOTE, AND THE DIFFERENCES BETWEEN THEM.

HISTORY

1846BC	1406	966BC	515BC	208.C.	69AD	1917	2005AD
ISAAC WEIR	JORDON CROSSED	TEMPLE STARTED	2 TEMPLE DEDICATED	3 TEMPLE STARTED	JERUSALEM BESEIGED	JERUSALEM FREED	TERMINUS AD QUEM
0	②	③	④	⑤	⑤	⑥	⑦
←440 YRS	440	440	451	495	88	1848	88
40×⑪	40×⑪	40×⑪	41×⑪	45×⑪	8×⑪	168×⑪	8×⑪
GEN. 21:8	JOSH. 5:10	1 KIN. 6:1	EZRA 7:22	HISTORY	LUKE 21:20	HISTORY	ZECH. 14:6

(DIA. 24)

GOD STAMPED THE NUMBERS 7 & 11 ON MUSIC, HISTORY & THE BIBLE. THEY ARE CONNECTED WITH SINGING, HARMONY, MUSIC, FEASTING AND DANCING. THE ABOVE HISTORICAL OCCASIONS ARE ALL CELEBRATION EVENTS OF GREAT JOY – NOT CONNECTED WITH BLOODSHED.
1 CHRON. 22:8

Chapter Six
The Metonic Cycle

"Mortals, congratulate yourselves that so great a man has lived for the honour of the human race."

"This inscription, on the tombstone of Sir Isaac Newton in Westminster Abbey, is a fitting tribute to the great Englishman who gave man new insight into the nature of the universe. For he demonstrated that the heavenly bodies scattered through space - comets, planets (including the earth) and meteors - are all part of the SAME system and that they all obey IDENTICAL mechanical laws. With almost unmatched mathematical genius, Newton proved that the same natural force that caused an apple to fall from a tree holds planets in their courses. We call this force of mutual attraction gravitation. Newton showed that gravitation acted in the SAME way throughout the universe. This is his theory of universal gravitation." (Pop. Science Vol. 3 p.278)

In Genesis 1 we read:-

"God made two great lights .... and God said .... let them serve as SIGNS to mark SEASONS and days and years." (v. 14-16 NIV)

In Psalm 89:37 we read :-

"It will be established forever like the moon, the faithful witness in the sky." (NKJV)

In Psalm 104:19 we read :-;

"He appointed the moon for the seasons."

In the 5th Century B.C. there lived in Athens a Greek astronomer named METON - he made the following discovery :-

"The earth, sun, and moon are in a straight line every 29.53 days. It so happens that 235 synodic months contain exactly the same number of days as 19 solar years; and therefore a particular phase of the moon will reoccur on the same calendar date every NINETEEN YEARS. So this period (known since 433 B.C. as the METONIC CYCLE) may well have been the means by which early man succeeded in combining two calendars."

(The Moon our Sister Planet Peter Cadogan)

In 'Times of the Signs' pages 146 - 153 we showed how the number NINETEEN in the Bible is connected with JUDGMENT, as Bullinger states :- "Nineteen is a number not without significance. It is a combination of 10 + 9 and would denote the perfection of divine order connected with JUDGMENT." ("Number in Scripture p. 262)

We clearly demonstrated with multiple bearings in our first book that the years 1999, 2002 and 2005 A.D. are connected with the greatest judgments that God will ever pour out on planet earth (Daniel 12:1 Matthew 24:21,34 Revelation 6-19).

The Nineteen Year Cycle (Dia. 25)

As the almost self-explanatory chart makes clear, plotting 19 year cycles from the time Solomon's Temple was commenced in 966 B.C., brings us through 156 cycles to 1999 A.D.! A time span of 2964 years whose factors are 3 x 4 x 13 x 19. The spiritual significance of these factors in combination would read like this 'The Complete Godhead (3) bringing judgment (19) on the earth (4) and Satan (13). For a fuller explanation of the spiritual significance of numbers get hold of the classic - 'Number in Scripture' by E.W. Bullinger, now back in print.

Sixty nine metonic cycles from the year the Moslems captured Jerusalem in 637 A.D. comes to 1948 when the State of Israel was re-established. Another 19 year cycle brings us to the Six Day War of 1967, when Israel

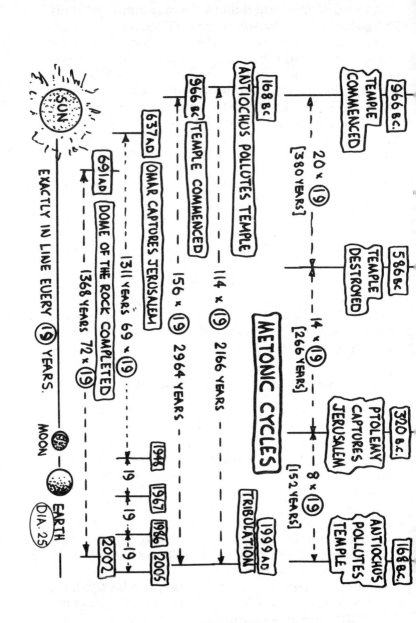

captured Eastern Jerusalem and the Temple Mount. Another 19 years and we arrive at 1986.

Halley's Comet

In 1986 Halley's Comet was in perihelion (nearest to the sun) on the 9th February (the author's 40th wedding anniversary!) Halley's Comet is the only brilliant comet that is predictable. It travels in an elongated egg shaped orbit, and its return period on average is 76 years i.e. 4 x 19! It was in aphelion (its furthest distance from the sun) in 1948 when Israel became a nation once more. This comet like the metonic cycle reminds us of the reoccurring 19 year cycle of prophetic crises.

Chernobyl Disaster 1986

On April 26th 1986 an explosion of the Chernobyl nuclear power station in South Western Russia sent a hundred million curies of radioactive material spewing into the air. It was the worst nuclear accident in history. As many as 200,000 people - perhaps more - will die of cancer as a direct result over the next fifty years. A book has been written by Drs Gale and Thomas Hauser entitled "CHERNOBYL THE FINAL WARNING."

Chernobyl means "wormwood" and this tragic warning foreshadows Revelation 8:10-11:-

"The third angel sounded his trumpet, and a great star, blazing like a torch, fell from the sky on a third of the rivers, and on the springs of waters - the name of the star is WORMWOOD. A third of the waters turned bitter, and many people died from the waters that had become bitter." (NKJV).

Another 19 year cycle from 1986 brings us to 2005 A.D.!, the terminus ad quem for man's control of planet earth. Man's lease on planet earth will shortly run out - the landlord (Jesus Christ) is returning shortly to take up a thousand year residence (Revelation 20:6). Before His return, He is putting the house that has been vandalised and polluted to the cleaners. Godless tenants will be permanently evicted, and only those who sign the new tenancy agreement will be able to live in the house during His Kingdom reign.

2002 A.D.

If our calculations are correct 2002 A.D. will trigger off the "Great Tribulation" of 3½ years, known as the "Time of Jacob's trouble." (Jeremiah 30:7, Zech. 13:8-9 etc). This will be caused by activities of Antichrist on the Temple Mount. On the Holy site of the Temple Mount, the Moslems completed their "Dome of the Rock" in 691 A.D. 72 metonic cycles, 1368 years from 691 A.D., lands us squarely in 2002 A.D. The 'Time' magazine for 16th October 1989 had more than a full page article on Jewish preparations for their new temple, which will be desecrated by Antichrist and trigger off the greatest anguish in Judea this world has ever known (Matthew 24:15-20).

Astronomy And Chronophecy

How marvellous that astronomy should point up the years 1999 A.D., 2002 A.D. and 2005 A.D. An expanded version of Genesis 1:14 would read :-

"The heavenly bodies are for a sign of something or someone to COME at the cycle of the set time or season I have appointed."

One of my most valued books is entitled "The Scripture Chronology demonstrated by Astronomical Calculations and also by the Year of Jubilee, and the Sabbatical Year among the Jews." It was printed 260 years ago in 1730 A.D. As they used acid free paper in those days it is in tip top mint condition. It measures 16" x 10" x 4" thick and is a veritable gold mine of chronological and astronomical information. The author was the Rev. Arthur Bedford M.A. His opening words are :-

"He who considers the exact motions of the heavenly bodies, and especially of the SUN and MOON, may thereby be fully convinced, that the orderer of them is a most wise and a powerful being; or, as we commonly say, that there is a God. And he who shall consider, how exactly these motions do correspond with several remarkable passages in the sacred scriptures, beyond all the possibility of human contrivance, cannot be equally sensible, that these scriptures were communicated to us by that God, who gave the laws of motion to these heavenly bodies; and that from the first creation of them, He infallibly foreknew whatsoever should come to pass in time, until the frame of this world shall be dissolved.''

On page 53 with exquisite sarcasm he writes :-

''It must be very admirable, that the heavens in their motions should enter into a confederacy with Moses to justify a chronology invented by him, unless the God who made the heavens, directed him what he should write.''

This book came into my possession just after 'Times of the Signs' was published - and it was a most satisfying confirmation to find that his time spans coincided exactly with mine!

The earth orbits the sun once every 365.2421 days. The square root of 365.2421 is 19.1113 - 19 nearest round number. So every year we have an annual reminder of the number NINETEEN!

Fighting The Stars

The heavenly bodies write in chorus with scripture and history, to proclaim in a deafening crescendo, the return of the Lord is near!! So very, very NEAR!!! Are you living your life, have you adjusted your relationships in the light of it? We read in Judges 5:20 *''Then fought the Kings of Canaan .... near the waters of MEGIDOO* (site of the last battle - Armageddon Revelation 16:12-16, 17:14, 19:17) .... *the STARS fought from heaven, from their courses they fought against Sisera.''*

Sisera was the army commander of Jabin the Canaanite King. He had a vastly superior army to

97

Israel's for he had nine hundred iron chariots (Judges 4:3) but in attacking Israel he was "fighting the stars." He was up against the Lord God Almighty. God sent heavy cloudbursts; the Kishon river rose, overflowing the plain, Sisera's horses and iron chariots became buried in the mud (Judges 5:21-22) just as Hitler's armour and heavy tanks were immobilised within just twenty kilometres of Moscow by God's all conquering army - MUD!

Stop "fighting the stars". The secret of success is to find which way God is moving, then go in that direction.

The Whitbread Round The World Yacht Race

When I wrote these lines in early January 1990 the third leg of the greatest yacht race in the world had just been completed in my home town Auckland N.Z. "the City of Sails". How thrilled and excited we were to have two New Zealand boats 1st and 2nd into harbour within six minutes of each other. For twelve days the two ketches - Steinlager 2 (Peter Blake) and Fisher and Paykel (Grant Dalton) had led the fleet, racing neck and neck 3,000 miles from Freemantle to Auckland.

On Friday morning, January 4th, excitement reached fever pitch as we observed on our T.V. screens the dramatic duel as they headed down the East Coast of the North Island towards Auckland. Steinlager 2 was only just in front. Fisher & Paykel, their rivals, about 30 nautical miles from the finish drew to within 200 metres. They could almost taste the victory champagne when disaster struck Grant Dalton's ketch. A last minute squall produced a violent 95 degree windshift. They were caught unawares. To avoid breaking the mainmast through slack sails, and a flogging spinnaker, they were forced to run off downwind - losing all chance of overhauling Steinlager 2.

Peter Blake's ketch was also hit by this sudden squall. Why were they not adversely affected? Well Peter Blake read the weather signs, and checked the Marine forecast on VHF radio, warning of a souwesterly wind change bringing winds gusting to 40 knots. The crew of Stainlager 2 quickly strapped down sails to cope with the same storm without being forced off-course. Peter Blake had read the signs, heeded the warning and won the race!

As *you* sail across the waters of life are you aware of the great storm just ahead? Are you reading the prophetic signs?

Hurricane Warning

In September 1938, a Long Island resident (New York) ordered from Abercrombie and Fitch an extremely sensitive barometer. When the instrument arrived at his home he was disappointed to discover that the indicating needle appeared to be stuck, pointing to the sector marked 'Hurricane.' After shaking the barometer vigorously several times - never a good idea with a sensitive mechanism - the new owner wrote a scathing letter to the store and, on the following morning, on the way to his office in New York, mailed it. That evening he returned to Long Island to find not only his barometer missing but his house as well. The needle of the instrument had been pointing correctly!

"Jesus said to the crowds! When you see a cloud rising in the West, immediately you say, 'It's going to rain', and it does. And when the south wind blows, you say, 'It's going to be hot,' and it is. Hypocrites! You know how to interpret the appearance of the earth and sky. How is it that you don't know how to INTERPRET THIS PRESENT TIME?"

(Luke 12:54-56 NIV)

Chapter Seven
That Sublime Number (37)

After the death of Solomon, the kingdom was divided (930 B.C.). Ten tribes formed the northern kingdom, called "Israel" with their capital at Samaria. It lasted 209 years until they were taken into captivity in 723 B.C. (Thiele) by the Assyrian King SHALMANESER (2 Kings 17:1-6). As Dia. 26 shows their chronoprophetic periods are all divisible by the number nine - the number of judgment.

The Kingdom Of Judah

Two tribes, Judah and Benjamin, formed the southern Kingdom called "Judah" with their capital at Jerusalem. It lasted 344 years until the Temple was destroyed in 586 B.C. by the Babylonians. (2 Kings 25:1-21). There are three steps in the progressive judgment on Judah.

1. DOMINATION (605 B.C.)
   Nebuchadnezzar conquered Jehoiakim, took temple treasures, and seed royal, including Daniel to Babylon (2 Chronicles 36:6-7 and Daniel 1:1-3).
2. DEPORTATION (597 B.C.)
   Nebuchadnezzar came again, and took the rest of the treasures, and King Jehoiachin, and 10,000 of the princes, officers and chief men, and carried them to Babylon (2 Kings 24:14-16).

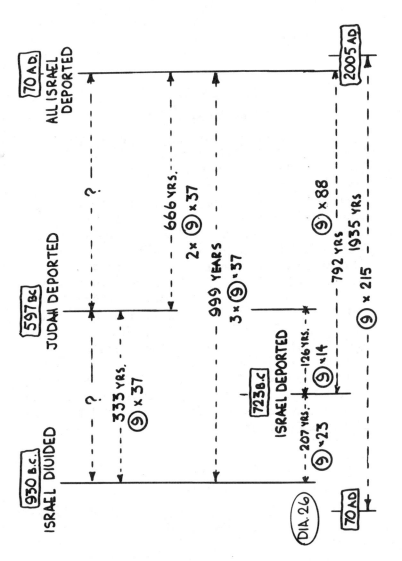

3. DESTRUCTION (586 B.C.)

The Babylonians came again, and burned Jerusalem, broke down its walls, put out the eyes of King Zedekiah, and carried him in chains to Babylon, with 832 captives, leaving only a remnant of the poorest class of people in the land. (2 Kings 25:8-12)

The Chronology Of The Southern Kingdom (Dia. 27)

Special blessings of leadership were prophesied by Jacob on his son JUDAH (Genesis 49:8-10, Matthew 2:6, Revelation 5:1-5) through the line of Judah came DAVID, DANIEL and the Lord Jesus Christ.

From the DIVISION of Israel in 930 B.C. to 597 B.C. when the bulk of Judah were deported to Babylon is exactly 333 years, or nine times thirty-seven. From the DEPORTATION to the DISPERSION in 70 A.D. is exactly 666 years, or eighteen times thirty seven - and of course from DIVISION to DISPERSION is 999 years or 27 x 37. These cycles of 37 years can be broken down still further - from the Deportation in 597 B.C. until the crowning of XERXES King of Persia (Esther 2:16) in 486 B.C. is 111 years or 3 x 37. From 486 B.C. to the crucifixion in 33 A.D. is 518 years or 14 x 37. From the cross to the fall of Jerusalem in 70 A.D. is exactly 37 years. And amazingly from the destruction of David's throne in 586 B.C. until 2005 A.D. is exactly 70 x 37!!! 2590 years, the times of the Gentiles!

Their Final Dispersion From The Land (Dia. 28)

Although the bulk of the nation were dispersed abroad by the Romans after 70 A.D. there were still sufficient Jews left in the land to put up a fierce resistance to the Roman conquerors of Masada in 73 A.D. After that, led by a Pseudo-Messiah BAR-KOCHBA (son of the star) they revolted again. When the rebellion was finally

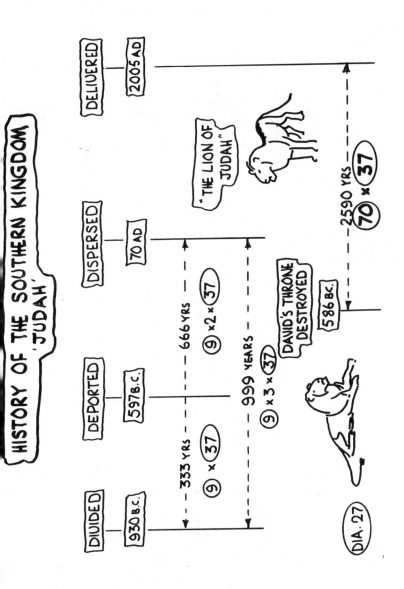

HISTORY OF THE SOUTHERN KINGDOM 'JUDAH'

DIVIDED — 930 B.C.
DEPORTED — 597 B.C.
DISPERSED — 70 AD
DELIVERED — 2005 AD

333 YRS — 9 × 37
666 YRS — 9 × 2 × 37
999 YEARS — 9 × 3 × 37

DAVID'S THRONE DESTROYED — 586 B.C.

"THE LION OF JUDAH"

2590 YRS — 70 × 37

DIA. 27

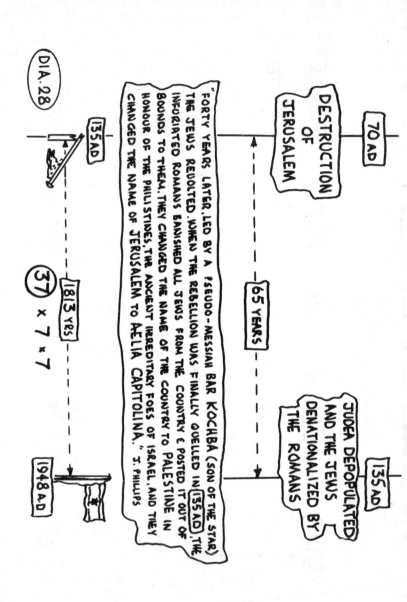

DIA.28

135AD

③⑦ × 7 × 7

1813 YRS

1948 A.D.

DESTRUCTION
OF
JERUSALEM

70AD

65 YEARS

JUDEA DEPOPULATED
AND THE JEWS
DENATIONALIZED BY
THE ROMANS

135 AD

"FORTY YEARS LATER, LED BY A PSEUDO-MESSIAH BAR KOCHBA (SON OF THE STAR),
THE JEWS REVOLTED. WHEN THE REBELLION WAS FINALLY QUELLED IN 135 A.D., THE
INFURIATED ROMANS BANISHED ALL JEWS FROM THE COUNTRY & POSTED IT OUT OF
BOUNDS TO THEM. THEY CHANGED THE NAME OF THE COUNTRY TO PALESTINE IN
HONOUR OF THE PHILISTINES, THE ANCIENT HEREDITARY FOES OF ISRAEL, AND THEY
CHANGED THE NAME OF JERUSALEM TO AELIA CAPITOLINA." J. PHILLIPS

104

quelled in 135 A.D. the infuriated Romans banished all Jews from the country and posted it out of bounds to them. They changed the name of the country to Palestine in honour of the Philistines, the ancient hereditary foes of Israel, and they changed the name of Jerusalem to AELIA CAPITOLINA.

The Jews were officially banished from their land from 135 A.D. until 1948 A.D. a period of 1813 years or 37 x 7 x 7! There are a number of other time spans of 37 years, but we will conclude with just two more. From the crossing into Canaan 1406 B.C. until the command to rebuild Jerusalem in 444 B.C. is 962 years or 26 x 37. And from 444 B.C. to 1999 A.D. is 2442 years or 66 x 37.

Incidentally 444 is a special number, it is exactly 12 x 37! 12 is the number of God's administration - and it was in 444 B.C. the command was given to start the 70 weeks of Daniel - the chronological vertebrate of prophecy. (See Appendix Two in "Times of the Signs"). 37 is also the 12th PRIME number.

From 637 A.D. when the Moslems captured Jerusalem until 2006 A.D. is 1369 years, which is exactly 37 x 37 years!

The Meaning Of The Number 37

Seeing all these cycles of 37 coming through the chronology of Judah I was convinced that it conveyed a special spiritual significance. Bullinger's book 'Number in Scripture' usually so helpful did not deal with this particular number. Thumbing through a book on numerics 'The Greatest Thing in the Universe' by Le Baron W. Kinney I found what I was searching for on page 151. In Daniel chapter 6 we learn how Darius had unwillingly put Daniel in the lions' den, and as a result spent a restless night worrying about Daniel's fate.

"At the first light of dawn, the King got up and hurried to the lions' den. When he came near the den, he called to Daniel in an anguished voice, "Daniel, servant of the living God, has your God whom you serve continually, been able to rescue you from the lions?"

Daniel answered "O King live forever! My God sent His angel, and he shut the mouths of the lions. They have not hurt me because I was found innocent in His sight." (Daniel 19-21 NIV)

The Chaldee word "God" in these verses has the numerical value of 37 - it is the number of the Godhead. But in New Testament Greek it is more specific, the name 'Jesus' has the value of 888 which equals 3 x 8 x 37, 'CHRIST' has the value of 1480 or 5 x 8 x 37.

How wonderful that through the chronological history of JUDAH - (the line of Christ) His name has been coded into all those time cycles that are multiples of 37! Truly He is *'KING OF THE AGES'* (Revelation 15:3-4).

The opening words of the Bible *"In the beginning God"* have the numerical value of 999 = 27 x 37! So we find the code name of Jesus Christ in the very first sentence of the Bible. Truly "Jesus Christ is the beginning of the creation of God" (Rev. 3:14).

We learnt how (Dia. 27) from 930 B.C. to 70 A.D. is 999 years or 3 x 9 x 37. This is highly significant. Jacob predicted *"The sceptre shall not depart from JUDAH, nor a lawgiver from between his feet, until Shiloh come"*

(Genesis 49:10).

F.J. Meldau says, "The word "sceptre" in this passage does not necessarily mean a King's staff. The word 'shebet' translated "sceptre" means primarily a "tribal staff". The TRIBAL IDENTITY of Judah shall not pass away - as did that of the other ten tribes - until Shiloh came.

For ages both Jewish and Christian commentators have taken "Shiloh" to be a name of Messiah. It means "Peace" or "one sent".

Even though Judah, during the seventy-year period of their captivity in Babylon, had been deprived of national sovereignty, they NEVER LOST THEIR "TRIBAL STAFF," THEIR NATIONAL IDENTITY, and they always had their own "lawgivers" (judges) of their own, even in captivity (Ezra 1:5,8).

At the time of Christ, though the Romans were

overlords of the Jews, the Jews had a king in their own land; moreover, they were to a large extent governed by their own laws, and the Sanhedrin of the nation still exercised its authority. But in the space of a few years, ARCHELAUS, the king of the Jews, was dethroned and banished. Coponius was appointed Roman Procurator, and the kingdom of Judah, the last remnant of the former greatness of the nation Israel, was formerly debased into a part of the province of Syria. For almost another half century the Jews retained the semblance of a provincial governmental structure; but in 70 A.D. both their city and their temple were destroyed by the armies of the Roman General Titus, and all semblance of Jewish national sovereignty disappeared. But the remarkable thing is this; Messiah (Shiloh) came BEFORE Judah lost its tribal identity, exactly as stated in Genesis 49:10!'' (Messiah in both Testaments p.30).

But 70 A.D. is not the end of Judah. The cycles of 37 in their history can be projected through to the end of the 70th week of Daniel in 2005 A.D. As we saw earlier from the fall of Jerusalem in 586 B.C. to 2005 A.D. is 2590 years or exactly 70 x 37!

For further information on the number 37 in Bible numerics I recommend :-

'The Seal of God' by F.C. PAYNE
P.O. Box 10 Strathpine
Queensland 4500 Australia
and/or
'God's Amazing Seal'
Te Awamutu
46 Spinley St
New Zealand

Mrs. Y. Broom
30 St. Matthews Street
Hull
HU3 2UA
U.K.

Chapter Eight

The Feasts Of The Lord
Leviticus 23

Israel had seven festivals which were all included within the first seven months of their religious calendar. They were held to a strict time schedule: *"These are the Lord's appointed feasts, the sacred assemblies you are to proclaim at the APPOINTED TIMES."* (Leviticus 23:4). The feasts were :-

1. The Passover (v. 4-5)
2. Unleavened Bread (v. 6-8)
3. The Sheaf of Firstfruits (v. 9-14)
4. The Feast of Pentecost (v. 15-21)
5. The Feast of Trumpets (v. 22-25)
6. The Day of Atonement (v. 26-32)
7. The Feast of Tabernacles (v. 33-43)

This sacred calendar is more than a list of holy days. It is actually an outline of God's calendar from eternity to eternity as Rabbi Hirsch explains:-

"The catechism of the Jew consists of his calendar. On the PINIONS OF TIME which bear us through life, God has inscribed the eternal words of His soul - inspiring doctrine, making days and weeks, months and years the heralds to proclaim His truths. Nothing would seem more fleeting than these ELEMENTS OF TIME, but to them God entrusted the care of His holy things, thereby rendering them more imperishable and more accessible than any mouth of priest, any monument, temple or altar could have done. Priests die, monuments decay, temples and altars fall to pieces, but TIME remains forever, and every newborn day emerges fresh and vigorous from its bosom." (Judaism Eternal vol.1 p.3)

The Passover: This was the initial Jewish feast and took place on the fourteenth day of the first month, NISAN (March-April) in their springtime. To the Jews it is a memorial of their mighty deliverance out of Egypt (Exodus 12). To the Christian it is a memorial type of our redemption *"Christ our Passover also has been sacrificed."* (1 Corinthians 5:7 cp. 1 Peter 1:19 NIV).

The Feast of Unleavened Bread: This feast speaks to us today of communion with Christ in the full blessing of His redemption and of a holy walk. It began on the fifteenth day of the first month Nisan and continued for a week.

The Feast of Firstfruits: This feast is typical of the resurrection of Christ. It was observed in the same week as the feast of unleavened bread, on the sixteenth day of Nisan. It is also typical of the believer's resurrection *"Christ the firstfruits, afterward, those who are Christ's at His coming."* (1 Corinthians 15:23 NKJV).

The Feast of Pentecost: This harvest feast is typical of the descent of the Holy Spirit to form the Church in Acts 2. Pentecost took place fifty days after the offering of the first fruits, coming at about the beginning of summer.

The Feast of Trumpets: This feast is a prophetic type and refers to the future regathering of long-dispersed Israel. Between the Feast of Pentecost and the Feast of Trumpets is the longest interval between any of the feasts. It was held on the first day of the seventh month, Tishri. (See Isaiah 27:12-13 and Joel 2:1-3:21)

The Day of Atonement: This looks forward to the repentance of Israel after their regathering in the land (Zechariah 12:10-14, 13:1). It was held on the tenth day of the seventh month, Tishri.

The Feast of Tabernacles: This feast looks forward prophetically to the Kingdom rest of Israel, after her regathering and restoration, when the feast becomes a memorial, not for Israel alone, but also for all nations (Ezra 3:4, Zechariah 14:16-21, cp. Revelation 21:3). It began on the fifteenth day of the seventh month, Tishri (our September/October) and lasted for one week.

Their Chronoprophetic Significance

Many writers have drawn attention to the rich spiritual teaching of these feasts that well repay earnest study, but our purpose is to point out the chronological prophetic significance of their TIME SEQUENCE.

Their calendar was based on the moon giving twelve thirty day months as we also find in Noah's calendar of the flood; also in Revelation 11:2-3 where the 42 months are equivalent to 1260 days 1260 ÷ 42 = 30 days. About every six years an extra month (second Adar or leap year month) was added because the calendar was based on the moon instead of the sun.

The Passover

"In the first month (Nisan), on the fourteenth day of the month ... is the Lord's passover."

How marvellous that Jesus Christ was crucified on this exact date! Hoehner in his book, "Chronological Aspects of Christ" p. 139 says "On Friday, Nisan 14, April 3, A.D. 33, Jesus was cut off or crucified." This is scripturally based on Daniel 9:26 with its precise mathematical prediction that from a command to rebuild Jerusalem (March 5, 444 B.C. Nisan 1) (Nehemiah 2:1-8) until Messiah would be cut off, would be after 69 weeks of 360 day years. 69 x 7 x 360 = 173,880 days. From 1st Nisan 444 B.C. if we add 173,880 days we come to Christ's triumphal entry on Nisan 10th A.D. 33 Monday March 30th (Luke 19:28-40). Four days later on the 14th Nisan He was crucified! Perfectly fulfilling the type of the Passover Lamb in Exodus 12 *"On the tenth day of this month (NISAN) they are each one to take a lamb to themselves"* (v. 3). *"And you shall keep it until the fourteenth day of the same month (NISAN) ... then kill it"* (v. 6). *"Behold the Lamb of God, who takes away the sin of the world."* (John 1:29 NKJV)

110

The Moon's Lunations

A lunation of the moon is the time from one new moon until the next new moon. I was interested to know how many lunations of the moon there were from the first Passover 1446 B.C. (Exodus 12) until *"Christ our Passover Lamb was sacrificed"* (1 Corinthians 5:7) in April 33 A.D. or 33.25 A.D. If we add $1446 + 33.25 - 1$ we obtain 1478.25 solar years. To convert to prophetic or moon years we simply do this:- $1478.25 \times 365.24 \div 360 = 1500$ lunations. Now $1500 = 12 \times 5 \times 5 \times 5$! i.e. in spiritual numbers - the Divine Administration (12) of complete grace ($5 \times 5 \times 5$). How wonderful it will be in the new heavens and the new earth when :-

"It shall be from NEW MOON to NEW MOON and from sabbath to sabbath, all mankind will come to bow down before me" (Isaiah 66:23 NASB). See also Isaiah 45:23, Romans 14:11 and Revelation 5:13.

The Feast of Firstfruits

This feast was held *"on the day after the Sabbath"* (Leviticus 23:11), that is the sixteenth day of Nisan - commemorating the resurrection of Christ on the first day of the week - Sunday. Hoehner says on page 143 "Christ was resurrected on Sunday, April 5th, 16th NISAN".

The Feast of Pentecost

From the feast of firstfruits they were commanded *"You shall count fifty days to the day after the seventh sabbath"* (Leviticus 23:16 NASB). From the sixteenth day of NISAN adding fifty days we come to the sixth day of their third month called SIVAN.

Exactly fifty days after Christ's resurrection we read *"and when the day of Pentecost had come, they were all together in one place"* (Acts 2:1). Individual Christian believers were for the first time baptised with the Holy Spirit into a unified spiritual organism, likened to a body of which Christ is the Head (1 Corinthians 12:12-13, Colossians 2:19).

This fourth feast is the only un-named feast in the twenty-third chapter of Leviticus. This is not without a good reason. The Church, the Body of Christ, was not seen in the Old Testament. It was "the mystery" (i.e. sacred secret) not made known in other ages to the sons of men, but was revealed to Paul by the Spirit (Ephesians 3:1-12).

These first four feasts were kept in the springtime and as we have seen they prefigure the death and resurrection of Christ, and the commencement of the Church. The yearly schedule of feasts for Israel now have the longest interval before we come to the last three feasts that anticipate Israel's regathering and glory.

The Feast of Trumpets

This feast is a prophetical type and refers to the future regathering of long dispersed Israel. *"You will be gathered up one by one, O sons of Israel. It will come about also in that day that a great trumpet will be blown."* (Isaiah 27:12-13 NASB)

"He will send forth his angels with a great trumpet, and they will gather together His elect (Israel, Deuteronomy 30:3, Isaiah 45:4) *from the four winds* (Daniel 7:2, Zechariah 2:6, Revelation 7:1) *from the one end of the heavens to the other"* (Matthew 24:31).

This feast was appointed for the first day of the seventh month TISHRI (September-October).

"Speak to the sons of Israel, saying, 'In the seventh month on the first of the month, you shall have a rest, a reminder by blowing of trumpets, a holy convocation.'" (Leviticus 23:24 NASB).

For a long time I was sure that this long span between the feasts of Pentecost and Trumpets indicated some hidden chronoprophetic significance. The beginning of the seventh millennium we found in "Times of the Signs" (p. 35) was 2005 A.D. We also know that the Day of Pentecost was Sunday, May 24 A.D. 33 (Hoehner p. 143). Thus the time span from A.D. 33 to A.D. 2005 is 1972 years. The span from the 6th SIVAN (PENTECOST) to the 1st TISHRI (TRUMPETS) is 116 days inclusive. "The Jews count both the beginning and ending day of a sequence" (New Scofield Bible p.16).

112

How could this relate to a time span of 1972 years? For five years, on and off, I had wrestled with this problem, then in March 1990 it became crystal clear.

The Prototype (Dia. 29)

These one hundred and sixteen days are twice fifty-eight days (twice is the essential double witness of Deuteronomy 19:15, Matthew 18:16) and fifty-eight if you remember in the 'S' Factory chapter, is the number of GRACE. "Noah's" name in Hebrew is made up of the number 8 + 50 = 58. The word GRACE is the word NOAH spelt backwards 50 + 8 = 58. The number 58 speaks of grace in many passages.

"Noah found grace in the eyes of the Lord." (Genesis 6:8)

The Chronoprophetic Fulfilment (Dia. 29)

Dividing the 116 days by 2 we came up with twice 58, a double witness to grace. If we divide the 1972 year span between 33 and 2005 A.D. into two, we come up with two more fifty-eights, speaking a double witness to grace not in days but in years. Not only does 58 crop up, but linked to it, praise the Lord, is that wonderful number seventeen! 58 x 17, 58 x 17 twice!! We learnt about the number seventeen when we studied the 'S' Factor chapter 4. "God assuring us on oath that the complete cycle of events He has ordered will be perfectly accomplished." But add to this symbolic meaning the number fifty-eight and what do we have?

58 x 17 is telling us twice, "God assuring us on oath that the complete cycle of events He has ordered will be perfectly accomplished *through His marvellous grace."*

"After Two Days" (Dia. 29)

Now 58 x 17 = 986 years; and we learnt in the Times of the Millenia that 986 solar years equal 1000 prophetic

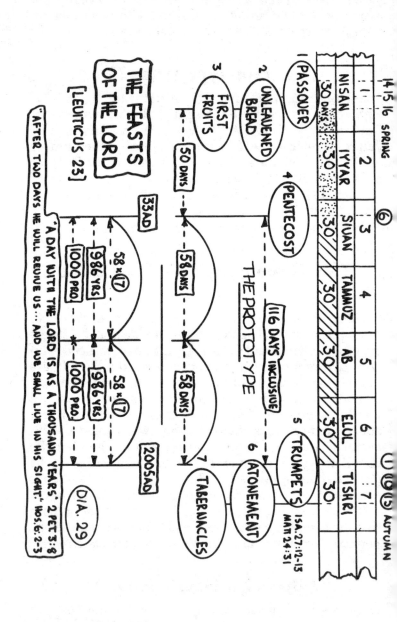

THE FEASTS
OF THE LORD

[LEVITICUS 23]

1 PASSOVER
2 UNLEAVENED BREAD
3 FIRST FRUITS
4 PENTECOST
5 TRUMPETS
6 ATONEMENT
7 TABERNACLES

THE PROTOTYPE

116 DAYS INCLUSIVE

50 DAYS
58 DAYS
58 DAYS
58 DAYS
58 DAYS

33AD
58 × 17
986 YRS
1000 PRO.

58 × 17
986 YRS
1000 PRO.

2005AD

DIA. 29

"A DAY WITH THE LORD IS AS A THOUSAND YEARS" 2 PET 3:8

"AFTER TWO DAYS HE WILL REVIVE US ... AND WE SHALL LIVE IN HIS SIGHT." HOS.6: 2-3

14 15 16 SPRING

1	2	3	4	5	6	7
NISAN	IYYAR	SIVAN	TAMMUZ	AB	ELUL	TISHRI
30 DAYS	30	30	30	30	30	30

ISA.27:12-13
MAT.24:31

AUTUMN

years! 986 x 365.24 ÷ 360 = 1000. Now *"a day with the Lord is as a thousand years"* (2 Peter 3:8 NKJV) and in Hosea we learn concerning the remnant of Judah *"He will revive us AFTER TWO DAYS; He will raise us up on the third day, that we may live before Him* (Hosea 6:20 NASB). After two days (2000 years) from crucifying the Lord of Glory 33 A.D. the remnant survivors will cry *"Come let us RETURN to the Lord. For He has torn us, but He will heal us; He has wounded us, but He will bandage us. He will revive us AFTER TWO DAYS; He will raise us up on the THIRD DAY that we may live before Him. So let us know, let us press on to know the Lord."* (Hosea 6:1-3 NASB). In the "third day", the millennium, Israel will be raised up to be the supreme nation amongst all the kingdoms of men *"The Lord will rise upon you, and His glory will appear upon you. And nations will come to your light, and Kings to the brightness of your rising."* (Isaiah 60:2-3 NASB)

Let us sum up this chapter with some helpful words from the late Harris Greg:-

"The feasts of the Lord (Leviticus 23) were God's annual clock in the tabernacle and temple. But, like the sun and solar system they were for signs as well as seasons (Genesis 1:14). The solar system is God's clock for earth, for our clocks and watches, for vegetation and animal life and for man's welfare. All light and time come from the heavens. The Lord's feasts were the clock of Christ and prophecy.

It was Passover when Christ died as the Passover Lamb of God, to take away, finally, the sin of the world. The clock pointed to 'the feast of first fruits' on the morning of His resurrection. It pointed to 'Pentecost' when He sent the Holy Spirit to gather His fruits, His exodus from Israel and all Gentile nations (Acts 2) for over nineteen centuries it has slowly moved toward 'The Feast of Trumpets', and Christ's return. Then it will point to 'The Day of Atonement' when, on the ground of Calvary, He will show Himself in His glory to Israel. He will be their glory, and Israel will be His glory (Luke 2:32, Isaiah 46:13). It will be His year of

Jubilee, and theirs. Then the clock will point to 'The Feast of Tabernacles', when Israel will bring all Gentiles to their Christ. The Garden and City of God will fill the earth with His glory, His love, and resurrection life and light. Then the clock will stop at the eternal 'sabbath of God's rest', in the new heaven and earth. *'There remaineth therefore a rest for the people of God.'* (Hebrews 4:9).''

Chapter Nine

1997 in Chronophecy

Pattern One

As we enter the final decade of this 20th century we can see a distinct pattern unfolding in connection with God's prophetic timepiece - the Jewish nation.

1. 1897 A.D. The first Zionist Congress was held at Basle, Switzerland, under the leadership of Theodore Herzel.

2. 1917 A.D. Exactly 20 years later the Turks were driven out of Jerusalem, the Balfour Declaration was signed and the Russian revolution occurred.

3. 1947 A.D. Exactly 30 years later the United Nations Organisation voted Israel a nation once more.

4. 1967 A.D. Exactly 20 years later, the Jews regained ALL of Jerusalem, that they had lost in 70 A.D. Surprisingly this is also exactly a time span of 1897 years! (1967-1897 = 70).

5. 1997 A.D. This will be exactly 30 years from 1967 A.D. Nothing of outstanding importance with Israel occurred in 1977 and 1987. But as God loves to work in specific patterns and cycles we can be sure 1997 A.D. is going to be an epoch making year with Israel. It is exactly 100 years from 1897 A.D. and precisely 2000 years from the birth of Christ in 4 B.C. Later we will see a number of time spans that lock into, converge and coincide exactly with 1997 A.D.

The Twenty - Thirty Pattern

These 20 - 30 - 20 - 30 year cycles from 1897 A.D. have a spiritual significance. As Bullinger has pointed out, 20 is one short of 21 (the three-fold seven) that denotes - complete (3) spiritual perfection (7). 20 signifies EXPECTANCY - this 20th century is eagerly expecting the 21st when the Kingdom of God will be established on earth.

Thirty, according to Bullinger, "being 3 x 10 denotes in a higher degree the perfection of Divine order as marking the RIGHT MOMENT."

Twenty years from 1897 the EXPECTANCY of the Zionists was fulfilled, when Jerusalem which had been held by the Turks for exactly 400 years, surrendered to British Forces in December 1917.

Thirty years later, at exactly the RIGHT MOMENT to the very day Nov. 29th 1947 (Times Signs pgs. 124-125) the U.N. Organisation voted Israel into existence!

For twenty years the young nation lived in eager EXPECTANCY of the day when all of Jerusalem would be in their hands. Right on time again, June 7th 1967 - Jerusalem was theirs!

As the cycle continues we can expect that again in thirty years time, at exactly the RIGHT MOMENT, a dramatic event will occur with Israel!

Pattern Two
God Playing At Sixes and Sevens
(Dia. 30)

When I am lecturing on this subject I ask, "Is there anyone here under 30 years of age who can tell me what the expression - 'at sixes and sevens' means?" There is always a dead silence! Older folks know that the expression refers to disorder, disarray, in a mess. But when God plays at sixes and sevens it is the exact opposite - ORDER, ORGANIZATION, SYN-CHRONIZATION.

Note in this marvellous pattern how all B.C. years end in a six - and all A.D. years end in a seven! In this self-explanatory pattern of interlocking, synchromesh years there are fourteen historical events that perfectly

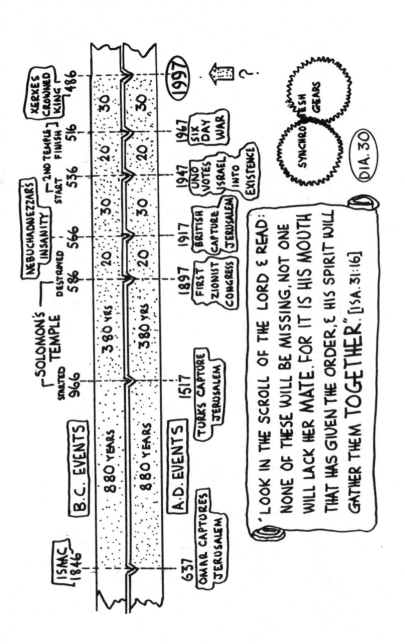

B.C. EVENTS

| ISMC 1846 | | SOLOMON'S TEMPLE started 966 | NEBUCHADNEZZAR'S INSANITY Destroyed 586 | 2ND TEMPLE start 536 / FINISH 516 | XERXES CROWNED KING 486 |

880 YEARS · 380 YRS · 20 · 30 · 20 · 30

OMAR CAPTURES JERUSALEM 637

A.D. EVENTS

880 YEARS · 380 YRS · 20 · 30 · 20 · 30 · 1997

TURKS CAPTURE JERUSALEM 1517

FIRST ZIONIST CONGRESS 1897

BRITISH CAPTURE JERUSALEM 1917

UNO VOTES ISRAEL INTO EXISTENCE 1947

SIX DAY WAR 1967

SYNCHRO MESH GEARS

DIA. 30

"LOOK IN THE SCROLL OF THE LORD & READ: NONE OF THESE WILL BE MISSING, NOT ONE WILL LACK HER MATE. FOR IT IS HIS MOUTH THAT HAS GIVEN THE ORDER, & HIS SPIRIT WILL GATHER THEM TOGETHER." [ISA. 31:16]

119

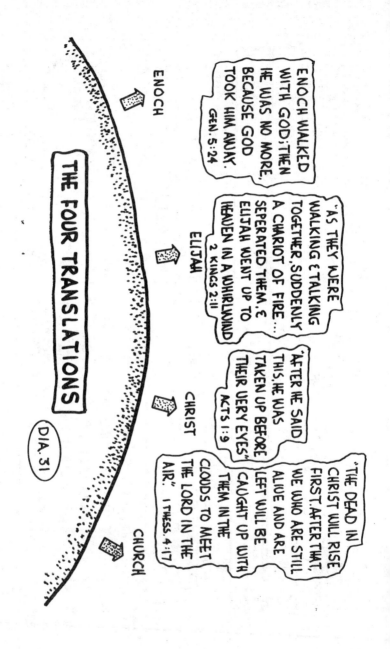

120

match their partners. The mathematical possibility of these events coinciding exactly in history, if it only happened by chance, beggars the imagination. The one who doubts they are face to face with God's design in history in this pattern is more credulous than the one who simply accepts the reality of historical facts.

How marvellous is the accuracy of chronophecy - what a marvellous guiding light as we draw near to the end of the journey. As Dr. Shadduck has well said, "If some mariner wishes to abolish the stars, and sail by a lantern hung in the rigging, he may do so, but not with my boat or my family". As we meditate on this marvellous union of B.C. with A.D. events, *"see to it that no one takes you captive through philosophy and empty deception, according to the tradition of men"*. (Colossians 2:8 NASB)

"What therefore God has joined together, let no man separate". (Matthew 19:6 NASB)

The Four Translations (Dia. 31)

This is not a discussion on the merits of various Bible translations; in my dictionary there are nine different meanings to the word 'translate'. We are discussing meaning no. 5 :-

"To convey or remove from one place to another, as a human being from earth to Heaven without natural death". (Funk & Wagnall)

1. Enoch
"Enoch walked with God; then he was no more, because God took him away". (Genesis 5:24 NIV)

2. Elisha
"As they were walking and talking together, suddenly a chariot of fire .... separated them and Elijah went up to Heaven in a whirlwind". (2 Kings 2:11 NIV)

3. Jesus Christ 33 A.D.
"After He said this, He was taken up before their very eyes". (Acts 1:9 NIV)

4. The Church - Known as the RAPTURE
"The dead in Christ will rise first, after that, we who are still

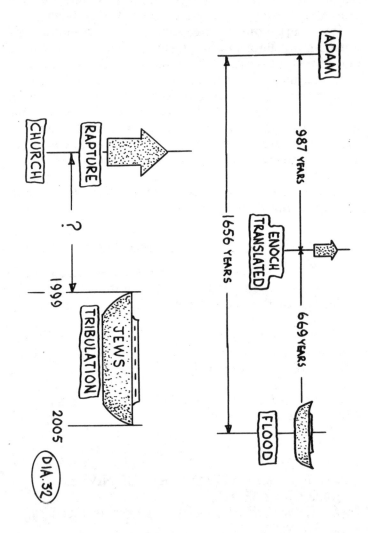

DIA. 32

CHURCH
RAPTURE
?
1999
TRIBULATION
JEWS
2005

ADAM
987 YEARS
ENOCH TRANSLATED
669 YEARS
1656 YEARS
FLOOD

alive and are left will be caught up with them in the clouds to meet the Lord in the air''. (1 Thessalonians 4:17)

Old prophetic writers consistently portray Enoch as a type of the Church being translated BEFORE Noah, a type of the Jewish remnant, who was protected through the flood waters of judgment i.e. the Tribulation.

My problem was how could one connect Enoch with the Rapture when he was translated 669 years before the flood? (Dia. 32)

At this stage of my quest the Holy Spirit was quickening my senses to accept the early Genesis chronologies just as they are written. In 'Times of the Signs' I had worked on the Old Testament text as far back as the birth of Abraham in 1951 B.C. However, as most Biblical scholars believe there are hidden gaps in the earlier genealogies I was reluctant to incorporate them into any scheme of chronophecy. (See App. 1 'Times of the Signs')

The Genesis Genealogies
(see back cover)

However, after reading Arthur Custance's book "Hidden Things of God's Revelation", I decided to accept them just as written, and when I did an astounding pattern emerged, which I will explain shortly. Arthur Custance has written at least nine volumes known as the "Doorway Papers". He holds an M.A. in Oriental Languages and a PhD. in Anthropology. On page 222, he writes :- "On the other hand, there are many of us who feel that to establish a relationship between the Lord as the last Adam and the First Adam, from whom we are all assumed to have been derived, by such a nonspecific and generalized family tree in which there are perhaps several hundred times as many names missing as are listed, is something less than satisfying. One feels that one is on solid ground when you read that Adam had a son whose name is Seth, and Seth had a son whose name was Enos, and Enos had a son whose name was Cainan, and so on through an unbroken chain of real people, many of whom are introduced to us in a way which makes them live even when we only have a single sentence about them. For such is the descriptive power of the Word of God.

So I think it makes good sense to take the Old Testament genealogies which supply the basis for the two genealogies found in Matthew and Luke with complete seriousness and assume that they mean what they seem to mean. It was the conviction of many of the older biblical chronologists that sufficient information was given in the Bible, not merely to establish this unbroken chain, but to set it within a quite precise time frame. It was the basis of course, of Ussher's chronology, which so many people today consider more the naive endeavour of a misinformed man than a serious contribution to understanding the Bible. But while Ussher's chronology may be in error in small details, it appears to me to encompass an overall view of the time span of man which is the right order of magnitude - though it is hopelessly in conflict with some modern Christian views. These modern views disagree with Ussher, and all those who have followed his approach to the problem, by arguing that the genealogies in Genesis are not intended to provide us with an unbroken chain. We are told again and again that some of these genealogies contain gaps; but what is never pointed out by those who lay the emphasis on these gaps is that they only know of the existence of these gaps because the Bible elsewhere fills them in. How otherwise could one know of them? But if they are filled in, they are not gaps at all! Thus in the final analysis the argument is completely without foundation. It is simply wishful thinking.''

He also points out :- ''The withholding of any time reckoning from those lines of descent which do not lead directly to the Promised Seed and the most precise enumeration of years in the line which does lead to the Saviour cannot be accidental.'' (p.224). This is an amazing phenomenon that TIME records were kept of

124

the Promised Seed by scribes who were unaware in the beginning whose family line was the seed! I would like to enlarge on this powerful evidence for the inspiration of the Scriptures, but we must not digress, except to say that Jesus Christ, in the genealogies, is the 77th from Adam. Anyone who is in tune with the spiritual significance of Bible numbers must rejoice at these two sevens - the number of spiritual perfection coming together in the Name of Jesus! (7 x 11) See Chap.5 'Sound of Music' for the spiritual significance on the number 'eleven'.

Publishing his excellent article in 1977 on the "Genealogies of the Old Testament" Custance makes this striking statement :- "I cannot believe that such detailed records from within a generation or two of Adam have been so perfectly preserved by accident. God had some purpose in mind : WE HAVE YET TO DISCOVER WHAT IT WAS." (p. 227 emphasis mine).

Well whatever other purpose they may or may not have, I have discovered that they are a marvellous key for unlocking some of the earliest secrets of chronophecy. What an exciting, thrilling, humbling experience it has been as the Lord has led me into this chronoprophetic goldmine.

"I make known the END from the BEGINNING, from ANCIENT TIMES what is still to come!" (Isaiah 46:10)

Accepting the genealogies as they stand we can address the question again, "How could Enoch connect with the Rapture when he was translated 669 years before the flood?"

Dating Enoch's Translation (Dia. 33)

At this stage the only one of the four translations we can accurately date is the ascension of our Lord on Thursday May 14th A.D. 33 (Hoehner). The time span in Genesis 5 from Adam to Enoch's translation is 987 years. The first glimmer of light came when I went from the known to the unknown. Adding 987 years to A.D. 33 gives us 1020 A.D. - but adding 987 years to 1020

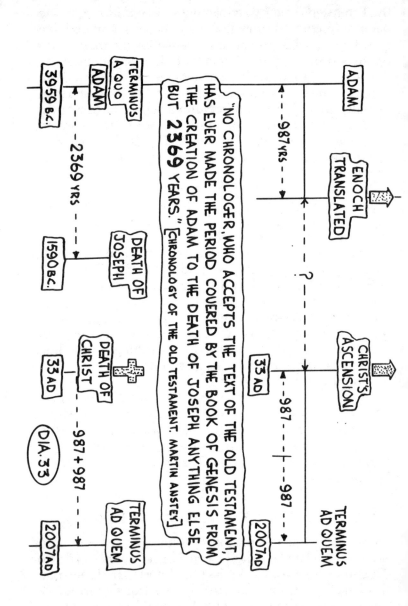

"NO CHRONOLOGER, WHO ACCEPTS THE TEXT OF THE OLD TESTAMENT, HAS EVER MADE THE PERIOD COVERED BY THE BOOK OF GENESIS FROM THE CREATION OF ADAM TO THE DEATH OF JOSEPH ANYTHING ELSE BUT **2369** YEARS." [CHRONOLOGY OF THE OLD TESTAMENT. MARTIN ANSTEY]

TERMINUS A QUO
ADAM
3959 B.C.

DEATH OF JOSEPH
1590 B.C.

2369 YRS

ADAM

987 YRS

ENOCH TRANSLATED

?

CHRIST'S ASCENSION

33 AD

987

987

2007 AD

TERMINUS AD QUEM

DEATH OF CHRIST
33 AD

987 + 987

TERMINUS AD QUEM
2007 AD

DIA. 33

126

A.D. brings us to 2007 A.D. which you will recall from pages 194/5 in 'Times of the Signs' is the commencement of the Great Sabbath Rest - the Millennium. Book 5 of the Psalms - as Church says "Yes, the fifth division of the Psalms (107 = 2007) implies the Logos period of world history - the millennial reign of Christ" (Hidden Prophecies in the Psalms p.20-21). Having found the terminus ad quem by adding 2 x 987 to 33 = 2007 A.D., can we now find the terminus a quo of redemptive chronology?

Finding The Terminus A Quo
(Dia. 34)

Martin Anstey in his book 'Chronology of the Old Testament' says on page 59 - "This is so mathematically exact and so absolutely certain, that since Ussher proved that Terah was 130 when Abram was born, no chronologer, who accepts the text of the Old Testament, has ever made the period covered by the book of Genesis from the Creation of Adam to the death of Joseph anything else but 2,369 years."

We demonstrated on page 122 of 'Times of the Signs' that Joseph was born in 1700 B.C. We learn from the last verse of Genesis that Joseph died at the age of 110 years. Therefore the year of his death is simply 1700 - 110 B.C. - 1590 B.C. Therefore adding 2,369 years to 1590 B.C. gives us the year 3959 for the creation of Adam. Our terminus a quo is therefore 3959 B.C. Working from this date, redemptive chronology comes alive. But first, let's answer two anticipated questions : 1. Why this 45 year gap from Ussher's date of 4004 B.C. if you accept the text of the Old Testament? Well until Prof. Thiele published his book in 1951 "The Mysterious Numbers of the Hebrew Kings", no one had successfully untangled the mass of chronological data of the Kings of Israel and Judah. Secondly the period of the Judges is difficult, but God's Word leap frogs that period in 1 Kings 6:1 giving us 480 years from

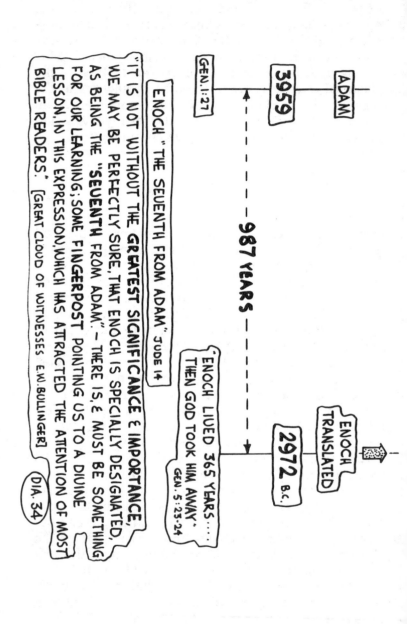

GEN.1:27

3959

ADAM

987 YEARS

"ENOCH LIVED 365 YEARS.....
THEN GOD TOOK HIM AWAY."
GEN. 5:23-24

2972 B.C.

ENOCH
TRANSLATED

ENOCH "THE SEVENTH FROM ADAM," JUDE 14

"IT IS NOT WITHOUT THE **GREATEST SIGNIFICANCE & IMPORTANCE,**
WE MAY BE PERFECTLY SURE, THAT ENOCH IS SPECIALLY DESIGNATED,
AS BEING THE "**SEVENTH** FROM ADAM".- THERE IS, & MUST BE SOMETHING
FOR OUR LEARNING; SOME **FINGERPOST** POINTING US TO A DIVINE
LESSON, IN THIS EXPRESSION, WHICH HAS ATTRACTED THE ATTENTION OF MOST
BIBLE READERS." [GREAT CLOUD OF WITNESSES E.W.BULLINGER]

DIA. 34

128

the Exodus 1446 B.C. to the start of Solomon's temple in 966 B.C.

2. How can you date Adam in 3959 B.C. in the light of evolution? Well personally I am not an evolutionist and have lectured extensively in the past on "Genesis and Geology". But irrespective of how long man has been on this earth, look on 3959 B.C. as the DATUM POINT, the terminus a quo of redemptive chronology.

An illustration might help. Whilst flying in Bomber Command in 1943 our squadron 214 was stationed at Chedburgh in East Anglia. It so happened that this was the highest point in Suffolk - several hundred feet above sea level, I think from a fading memory about 700 feet above sea level. Our altimeter which records our altitude was never set at take off at zero (sea level) but at 700 ft. 700 ft. was *our* sea level! That was our datum point - imagine trying to land 700 ft. below the runaway! So look on 3959 B.C. as the DATUM POINT of redemptive chronology, and then, and only then will you see the wonderful prophetic patterns emerge from these early genealogies. Remember *"I make known the END from the BEGINNING, from ANCIENT TIMES what is still to come"*. (Isaiah 46:10 NIV).

Plotting 987 years from Adam 3959 B.C. we come to the year (3959 - 987) 2972 B.C. for the translation of Enoch (Dia. 34). Now if Enoch and the flood are types of the Rapture and the Tribulation how do they tie up with chronophecy?

Could This Be The Rapture Year?

For years I have insisted that the Rapture is an undatable event, but now I wonder. Moving with studied reserve I cannot conceal any longer the chrono-prophetic truths of Scripture in this connection. First of all, and this may come as a bit of a shock to Christians who *"love His appearing"* - there is not a single verse in the Bible prohibiting anyone from dating the Rapture even to the day, hour, minute and second if they so desire! Every reference in the Olivet Discourse

(Matthew 24/25) to *"no one knows the day nor the hour"* refers to the *"Son of Man"* coming at the SECOND ADVENT - not the RAPTURE!

There seems to be a growing awareness amongst Christians that 1997 A.D. *could* be the year of the Rapture. Christ came in 4 B.C. to earth, but only to those in the 'know'. He was not publicly manifested to the world until later. Now 2,000 years from 4 B.C. brings us to A.D. 1997 exactly. (2000 - 4 + 1 = 1997) that is only one bearing, and as a navigator did not convince me on its own. Were there any more clues - how could Enoch's translation be connected even remotely with 1997 A.D.?

Enoch And The Rapture (Dia. 35)

I measured the time span from his translation in 2972 B.C. to A.D. 1997 it is 4968 solar years. Try as I may, this figure did not have any apparent prophetic connection with A.D. 1997. But when I converted to prophetic years - all the pennies dropped!!

4968 x 365.24 ÷ 360 = 5040 years.

I decided to factorize this number as it still did not mean anything to me, so I started with the lowest number and divided 5040 by 2 - on the little screen of my pocket calculator - up flashed the figures 2520! I could hardly believe my eyes, I rechecked all the calculations it couldn't be, but it wouldn't go away, 2520 prophetic years!!

2520 In Chronophecy

If you are not aware of the prophetic importance of 2520 let me quote from Bullinger :-

"There are four so-called perfect numbers, 3, 7, 10 and 12.

3 is the number of Divine Perfection.

7 is the number of Spiritual Perfection.

10 is the number of Ordinal Perfection.

12 is the number of Governmental Perfection.

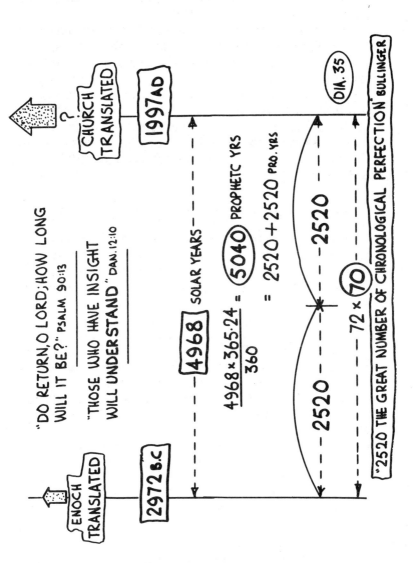

"DO RETURN, O LORD; HOW LONG
WILL IT BE?" PSALM 90:13

"THOSE WHO HAVE INSIGHT
WILL UNDERSTAND." DAN. 12:10

ENOCH TRANSLATED   2972 B.C.

CHURCH TRANSLATED   1997 AD

4968 SOLAR YEARS

$$\frac{4968 \times 365 \cdot 24}{360} = 5040 \text{ PROPHETIC YRS}$$

$$= 2520 + 2520 \text{ PRO. YRS}$$

2520

2520   2520

72 × 70

DIA. 35

"2520 THE GREAT NUMBER OF CHRONOLOGICAL PERFECTION" BULLINGER

131

The product of these four perfect numbers forms the great number of CHRONOLOGICAL PERFECTION. 3 x 7 x 10 x 12 = 2520.

It is the least common multiple (L.C.M.) of all the ten numbers from which our systems of notation is derived; for the L.C.M. of 1,2,3,4,5,6,7,8,9,10, is 2520'' (Number in Scripture p. 23/24).

The waypoints in Chapter 5 of ''Times of the Signs'' demonstrated how many times this number is connected with prophetic crisis years in history.

Two time spans of this wonderful number from Enoch's translation B.C. 2972 lands us squarely in 1997 A.D. i.e. in prophetic years. This double 2520 is in keeping with the concept of TWO witnesses as establishing a point (Deuteronomy 19:15, Matthew 18:16, 2 Corinthians 13:1). In Daniel 12:7 the angel, to emphasise the solemnity of the oath, raised BOTH hands. Ordinarily, only one hand was raised. (Genesis 14:22, Deuteronomy 32:40).

5040 prophectic years is also exactly 72 x 70, that great measuring span in prophecy.

Enoch And 2005 A.D.

We have just seen how 5040 prophectic years from Enoch's translation (2972 B.C.) comes to 1997 A.D. Now another amazing fact emerges if we measure 5049 prophetic years from 2972 B.C. Why 5049? Well that is exactly 33 x 153 (3 x 11 x 9 x 17) Remember the number 153 in the 'S' factor, how it came so marvellously to 2005 A.D.? 33 x 153 prophetic years is 5049 prophetic years, converting to solar 5049 x 360 ÷ 365.24 is 4976 years. If we add 4976 years to Enoch's translation in 2972 B.C. up comes our well established number 2005 A.D.!!

Enoch And 2520

Bullinger in his book on Hebrews 11 says in regard to Enoch, ''It is not without the GREATEST

SIGNIFICANCE and IMPORTANCE we may be perfectly sure, that Enoch is specially designated as being the "SEVENTH from ADAM" there is, and must be something for our learning; some FINGERPOST pointing us to a divine lesson, in this expression, which has attracted the attention of most Bible readers." (Great Cloud of Witnesses p.79)

If we put together the two numerical facts about Enoch "the SEVENTH from Adam" (Jude 14) and "Enoch lived 365 years" (Genesis 5:23) then apply the prophetic year of 360 days - look what happens -

$365 \times 360 \div 365 = 360$ years
$360 \times 7 \qquad = 2520$ years
$\qquad \qquad = 36 \times 70$

If we change the ratio another amazing fact emerges

$365 \times 365 \div 360 = 370$ years
$370 \times 7 \qquad = 2590$ years
$\qquad \qquad = 37 \times 70$

So hidden away in these two figures of 7 and 365, by simply introducing the prophetic year of 360 days we have :-

1. 2520 the number of chronological perfection.
2. 2590 - The Times of the Gentiles from 586 B.C. to 2005 A.D.
3. 37×70 37 the number of Jesus Christ.
    70 the basic measuring unit.

What marvellous chronoprophetic facts are tucked away in these simple biographical facts of Enoch, waiting to be uncovered in these end times :- *"From now on I will tell you of NEW things, of HIDDEN things unknown to you"*. (Isaiah 48:6-8 NIV).

Where Does Noah Fit In? (Dia. 36)

19th Century prophetic writers consistently pictured Noah as a type of the spared remnant of Israel preserved through the Tribulation and Enoch translated before as a clear type of the Pre-Tribulation Rapture. How does chronophecy tie up these thoughts with mathematical precision? It does it in three ways :-

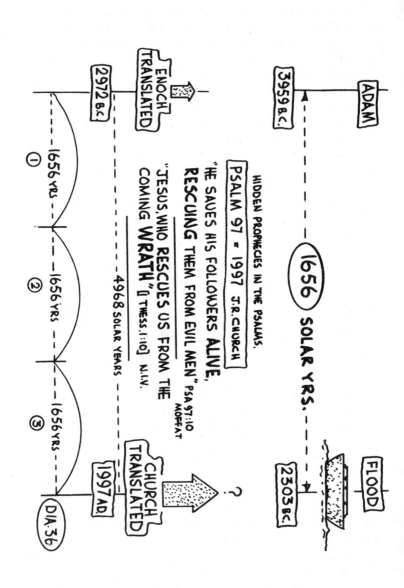

HIDDEN PROPHECIES IN THE PSALMS.

PSALM 97 = 1997 J.R.CHURCH

"HE SAVES HIS FOLLOWERS ALIVE,
RESCUING THEM FROM EVIL MEN" PSA 97:10
MOFFAT

"JESUS,WHO RESCUES US FROM THE
COMING WRATH" [I THESS.I:10] N.I.V.

4968 SOLAR YEARS

2972 B.C.

ENOCH
TRANSLATED

① 1656 YRS

② 1656 YRS

③ 1656 YRS

1997 A.D.

DIA.36

CHURCH
TRANSLATED

?

3959 B.C.

ADAM

1656 SOLAR YRS.

FLOOD

2303 B.C.

134

1. We have demonstrated that twice 2520 prophetic years lands us in A.D. 1997.

2. The time span from Adam B.C. 3959 to the flood in B.C. 2303 is 1656 years. If we use 1656 solar years as a time cycle another amazing pattern emerges. Measuring three (the number of completeness) times 1656 years from Enoch's translation in 2972 B.C. we come unerringly into the year A.D. 1997!! Which if it is the year of the Rapture, links it with chronological perfection to Enoch's translation! (Dia. 35) 2656 x 3 = our three witnesses Matthew 18:16

3. How can the flood be linked with the Tribulation A.D. 1999? (See 'J' factor in ' Times of the Signs'). Well the flood occurred in 2303 B.C. (Dia. 36). Measuring from the flood to A.D. 1999 we have a period of 4301 years which is perfectly divisible by 17 (17 x 253 = 4301).

God had shut Noah safely in the Ark when the flood waters burst upon an unsuspecting world and *"on the seventeenth day of the month"* (Genesis 7:11) 17 was a sweet number to Noah, as God had SHUT HIM IN THE ARK. But to the ungodly it was a dreadful, frightening number because they were SHUT OUT!

From 1897 (first waypoint to the end) until A.D. 1914 (First World War commenced) is 1 x 17 years. From 1914 to 1948 (first Israeli war) is 2 x 17 years. From 1948 to 1999 A.D. (Tribulation worldwide) is 3 x 17 years.

One! Two! Three! *"I will overturn, overturn, overturn, it; and it shall be no more, until he come whose right it is; and I will give it to him"*. (Ezekiel 21:27)

"Hidden Prophecies In The Psalms"

In the epilogue to 'Times of the Signs' we drew attention to J.R. Church's book 'Hidden Prophecies in the Psalms' in which he teaches that each Psalm represents a year this century e.g. Psalm 17 = 1917, Psalm 48 = 1948. On this basis I returned to Psalm 97 = 1997 to see if there was any clue to the Rapture in that year. It was rather startling to read these words in Psalm 97:10 :-

"He saves His followers ALIVE, RESCUING them from EVIL men" (Moffatt Trans.)

These words have a familiar New Testament ring about them:-

"We which are ALIVE and remain shall be CAUGHT UP together .... to meet the Lord in the air: and so shall we ever be with the Lord." (1 Thessalonians 4:17)

"We shall not all DIE, but we will all be changed - in a flash, in the twinkling of an eye, at the last trump." (1 Corinthians 15:51-52)

"Jesus who RESCUES us from the coming WRATH". (1 Thessalonians 1:10 NIV)

What joy, what hope, what comfort is the glorious pre-Tribulation Rapture of the saints!

Bible Numerics and A.D. 1997

An Arab Christian ANIS SHORROSH in his book "Jesus, Prophecy, and the Middle East", explains what Jesus meant when He said, *"Jerusalem will be trampled under foot by the Gentiles".* (Luke 21:24).

He says :- "In Hebrew the phrase "trampled underfoot by the Gentiles" is Yerushalem Tel, meaning Jerusalem will become a heap. Archaeologists use the term 'tel' so commonly that most everyone knows its meaning immediately. 'Tel', a man-made mound, refers to the historic practice of conquering armies who would plunder and burn a city, leaving all the remains in a heap of rubble.

In time weeds and scrub brush take over such a site, and with the passing of more time, all that survives is a mound. In the last two centuries hundreds of these tels have yielded to the picks and shovels of the archaeologists, opening up hidden treasures and revealing much about life in earlier times. Jesus prophesied that Jerusalem would become Yerushalem Tel.

The Hebrew alphabet numbers twenty-two characters and each has a numerical significance. The letter aleph is the figure 1, beth is 2, givel is 3 - and so on. When the value of the characters in a word of phrase is summed up, if often conveys a HIDDEN meaning - given DATE, or the number in an army or an amount of gold.

When Jesus said Gentiles would make a heap of Jerusalem, His listeners could have determined the EXACT YEAR this would happen if they had added up the equivalent value of the words YERUSHALEM TEL. The sum of these letters is 3830 or, when translated into the chronology of the Gregorian calendar, A.D. 70! Thus Jesus provided His listeners with the precise year of Jerusalem's destruction and the Jewish dispersion. History and biblical prophecy compliment each other because history is actually His story''. (p. 77/78)

I checked out the Jewish calendar.

A.D. 1948 was the Jewish year 5708

- A.D. 70 - 1878

= 1878 = 3830.

Therefore A.D. 70 = 3830 Jewish time. You say what has all this to do with A.D. 1997? Well Shorrosh has shown that dates are hidden in the numerical structure of the Bible. Like Hebrew, the Greek of the N.T. also has a numerical value for each letter of its alphabet.

The Old Testament closes with Malachi's prophecy to Israel (1:1) and in Chapter 4:2 we read of the *"Sun of righteousness rising with healing in his wings"* (for Israel - context) but the New Testament closes with the *"bright Morning Star"* coming for His Church. As the morning star is seen well before sunrise so the Rapture will precede the Second Advent.

In Peter we read, *"We have a more sure word of prophecy in which you do well to take heed, as a lamp shining in a dark place, until the day dawns, and the DAYSTAR rises in your hearts."* (2 Peter 1:19) Jay Green's translation.

The numerical value of DAYSTAR in Greek is 2440. The great datum point of the seventy weeks of Daniel is 444 B.C. (Nehemiah 2:1-8 and Daniel 9:25). If we measure 2440 years from 444 B.C. we come once more to A.D. 1997. Just one more bearing suggesting a 1997 Rapture. (Dia. No. 37)

If we measure from Nebuchadnezzar's accession to

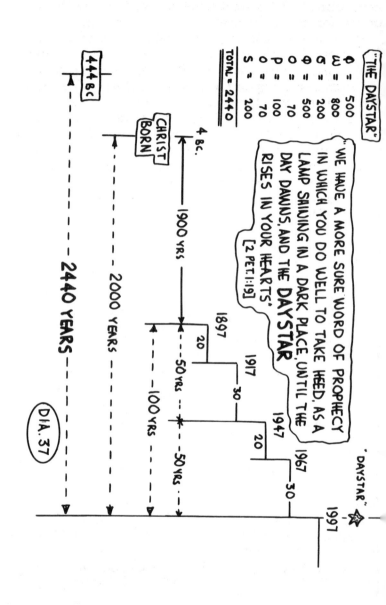

"THE DAYSTAR"

D = 500
W = 800
S = 200
T = 500
O = 70
P = 100
O = 70
S = 200

TOTAL = 2440

"WE HAVE A MORE SURE WORD OF PROPHECY IN WHICH YOU DO WELL TO TAKE HEED, AS A LAMP SHINING IN A DARK PLACE, UNTIL THE DAY DAWNS, AND THE DAYSTAR RISES IN YOUR HEARTS."
[2 PET.1:19]

444 B.C.

CHRIST BORN

4 B.C.

1900 YRS

1897
20
50 YRS
1917
30

1947
20
50 YRS
1967
30

100 YRS

2000 YEARS

2440 YEARS

DIA. 37

"DAYSTAR"

1997

the throne in B.C. 605 through to A.D. 1997 we have a time span of 2601 years which is 153 x 17! (See under 'S' Factor for its importance).

We read of a "morning star" again in Revelation 2:26-28 but its context is the millenial reign of Christ. *"To him who overcomes and does my will to the end, I will give authority over the nations - He will rule them with an iron sceptre; he will dash them to pieces like pottery - just as I have received authority from my Father, I will also give him the MORNING STAR".*

The numerical value of "THE MORNING STAR" in Greek is 2607. Now the first year of Nebuchadnezzar's reign was 604/603 B.C. (see p. 99 'Times of the Signs'). 2607 years on from B.C. 603 comes to A.D. 2005! The end of the times of the Gentiles!

Chapter Ten

The Chronopropheticscope (Dia. 38)

Imagine an instrument like a theodolite through which we could place the plumb-line over an ancient historic event and measure to another plumb-line in our time. Having measured the distance in solar years, we then extend it on the prophetic ratio - the results are amazing to say the least. The two key dates in our time are:

1. May 14th 1948 (rebirth of Israel) that is 1948.36 solar years.

2. June 7th 1967 (capture of Temple Mount) that is 1967.43 solar years.

Let us place our imaginary chronopropheticscope on the birth of Abraham 1951 B.C. then measure the time in solar years to a plumb-line placed on 1948.36 A.D. and the distance in years equals 3898.36 solar. Now press the lever on our "chronopropheticscope" to extended prophetic and the reading on the "dial" is 3898.36 x 365.24 ÷ 360 = 3955.10 years. If we add 3955.10 to 1951 B.C. we have (3955.10 - 1951 + 1) 2005.10 A.D.!

Let us now place the plumb-line on 624 B.C. (the rise of Babylon), measure the time to the Six Day War 1967.43 A.D. and it is (624 + 1967.43 - 1) 2590.43 years. Extend the prophetic ratio "lever" (2590.43 x 365.24 ÷ 360 = 2628.1 years), add this to 624 B.C. (2628.13 - 624 + 1) and we have 2005.1 A.D.!!

In "Times of the Signs" we came up with the year 2001 B.C. when Joseph made himself known to his brethren - this was based on the typology of Genesis 45:6-7 (p.122-123). Let us now check this out with our "chronopropheticscope". Place its plumb-line over 1700 B.C. when Joseph was born, measure to 1948.36

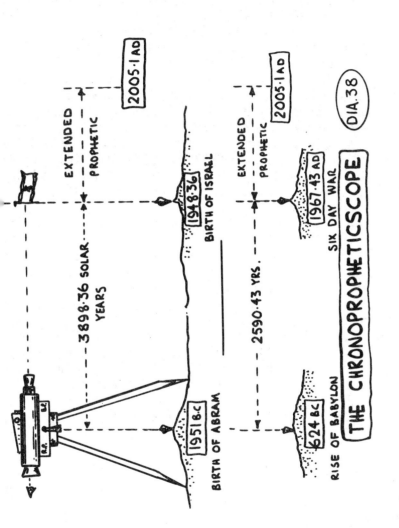

EXTENDED PROPHETIC

2005·1 AD

3898·36 SOLAR YEARS

BIRTH OF ISRAEL — 1948·36

BIRTH OF ABRAM — 1951 B.C

EXTENDED PROPHETIC

2005·1 AD

2590·43 YRS.

SIX DAY WAR — 1967·43 AD

RISE OF BABYLON — 624 BC

THE CHRONOPROPHETICSCOPE

DIA.38

141

A.D. and it comes to (1700 + 1948.36 - 1) 3647.36. Now press the "lever" to extended prophetic and the reading on the dial is (3647.36 x 365.24 ÷ 360) = 3700.44 years, add this to 1700 B.C. and we have (3700.44 - 1700 + 1) equals 2001.4 A.D.!!

Let us apply the chronopropheticscope to our findings about Jacob in "Times of the Signs" (p.119-120) we come up with the year 2002 A.D. for the start of "Jacob's trouble" - the Great Tribulation. Place the plumb-line over Jacob's birth year 1791 B.C. and measure to 1948.36 A.D. The time span is (1791 + 1948.36 - 1) 3738.36 years. Now press the "lever" for extended prophetic, and the reading on the dial is (3738.36 x 365.24 ÷ 360) 3792.77 years. Add this to 1791 B.C. and we have (3792.77 - 1791 + 1) 2002.77 A.D.!! Thus we have two amazing confirmations of Joseph and Jacob by our highly "scientific" chronopropheticscope. Note, although it is an imaginary instrument, its calculations are REAL.

Just one more peep through the scope. In the "Times of Moses" p.127 in "Signs of the Times", we worked on 1999 A.D. as the beginning of the Tribulation. Let's check it out - place the plumb-line over Moses' birth year 1526 B.C. and measure to 1948.36 A.D. the time span is (1526 + 1948.36 - 1) 3473.36 years. Now press the lever for EXTENDED PROPHETIC and the reading on the dial is (3473.36 x 365.24 ÷ 360) 3523.9 years. Add this to 1526 B.C. (3523.9 - 1526 + 1) and we have 1998.9 A.D. or 1999 to the nearest round number!! Many more examples could be shown, these examples are just to encourage you to take a 'peep' for yourself.

Chapter Eleven

The Tents Of Abraham
(Dia. Nos. 39 and 40)

What possible connection could there be between
Abraham living a quiet leisurely life in tents, with the
hurly-burly of Babylon and the destruction of Jerusalem
and Solomon's temple? How could this shepherd be
linked with the Moslem capture of Jerusalem and the
building of the EL-ASKA Mosque on the Temple
Mount? What is the tie-up with a nomad from the 20th
century B.C. with all the startling events connected
with Israel's restoration in the 20th century A.D.? How
can we couple up events nearly 4,000 years apart? As
staggering and incredible as it may seem, they are
chronologically programmed into a series of events,
based on biblical and astronomical time scales from the
call of Abraham in 1876 B.C. until the return of Jesus
Christ. For an explanation of the time scales refer to
Appendix No. 1 (Dia. 50).

The Babylonian Era (Dia. 41)

In 1876 B.C. Abram at the age of 75 heard the call of
God and departed from Haran (Genesis 12:1-4). If we
measure 1290 lunar years (354.36 days per year) from
1876 B.C. we come to 624 B.C. - the rise of the
Babylonian Empire. Measuring 1290 prophetic (360
days per year) we come to 605 B.C. when King
Nebuchadnezzar acceded to the throne. Measuring
1260 extended prophetic years brings us to 597 B.C.
when the bulk of the population of Jerusalem was taken

143

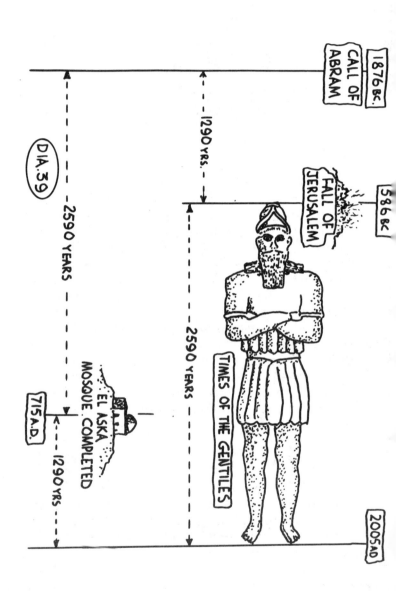

1876 B.C. CALL OF ABRAM

1290 YRS.

DIA. 39

2590 YEARS

586 B.C. FALL OF JERUSALEM

2590 YEARS

TIMES OF THE GENTILES

EL ASKA MOSQUE. COMPLETED

715 A.D.

1290 YRS.

2005 A.D.

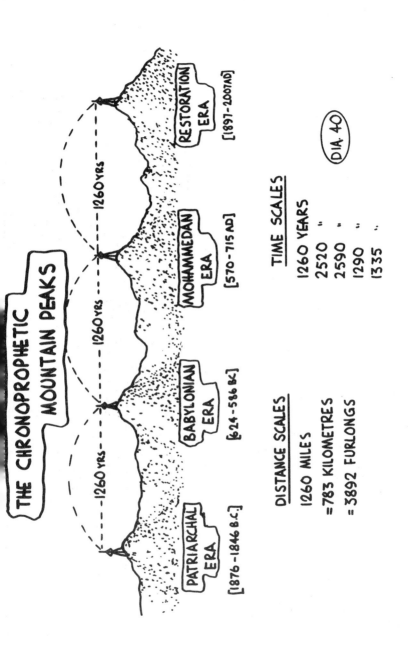

THE CHRONOPROPHETIC MOUNTAIN PEAKS

PATRIARCHAL ERA [1876-1846 B.C.]

BABYLONIAN ERA [624-586 B.C.]

MOHAMMEDAN ERA [570-715 AD]

RESTORATION ERA [1897-2007AD]

1260 YRS

1260 YRS

1260 YRS

DISTANCE SCALES

1260 MILES
= 783 KILOMETRES
= 3892 FURLONGS

TIME SCALES

1260 YEARS
2520 "
2590 "
1290 "
1335 "

(DIA. 40)

145

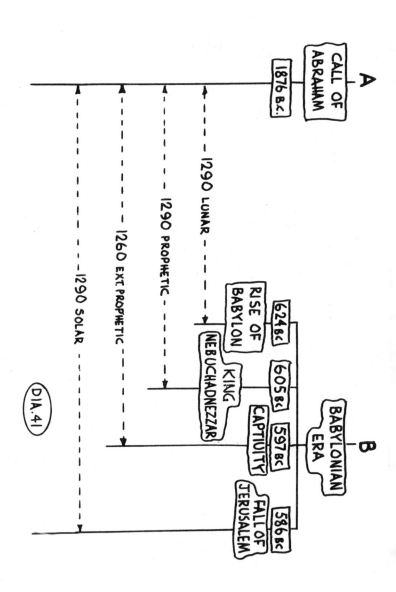

DIA. 41

Diagram showing timeline from A (Call of Abraham, 1876 B.C.) to B (Babylonian Era):
- 1876 B.C. – Call of Abraham
- 1290 Lunar
- 1290 Prophetic
- 1260 Ext Prophetic
- 1290 Solar
- 624 B.C. – Rise of Babylon
- 605 B.C. – King Nebuchadnezzar
- 597 B.C. – Captivity
- 586 B.C. – Fall of Jerusalem
- Babylonian Era

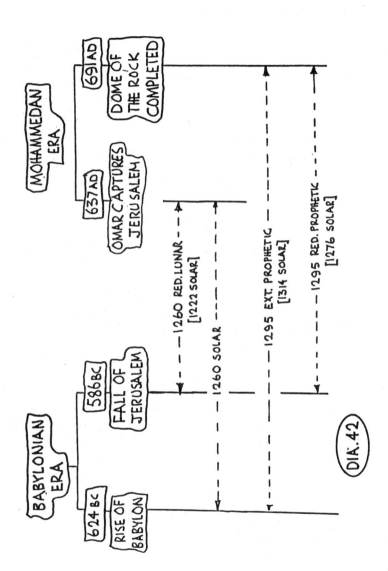

DIA. 42

into captivity. Measuring 1290 solar years from 1876 B.C. we come to that critically historic year 586 B.C. when Jerusalem and Solomon's temple were destroyed.

The Mohammedan Era (Dia. 42)

If we measure 1260 solar years from the rise of Babylon in 624 B.C. we come to 637 A.D. when Omar captured Jerusalem. Measuring 1295 extended prophetic years brings us to that key year 691 A.D. when the Dome of the Rock was completed. Measuring 1260 reduced lunar years from the fall of Jerusalem in 586 B.C. we come to 637 A.D. again! 1295 reduced prophetic years from 586 B.C. bring us to 691 A.D. again!!

The Restoration Era (Dia. 43)

From 1897 A.D. we have the vital events that lead to Israel's full restoration and the setting up of the Kingdom Age by 2007 A.D.

A glance at Dia. 43 shows ten time spans chrono-prophetically linked between key Mohammedan and Jewish events - Ishmael and Isaac. God has given us these many exact time spans to guide us and warn us how close we are to the end of this age prior to Christ's return. As a ship enters the entrance to a harbour, flashing beacons guide it along the last stretch before berthing. In 1897 A.D. (first Zionist Congress) the warning beacons started flashing and so on through 1917, 1947 etc. We are approaching journey's end. Are you ready to disembark? Are all your papers all in order? Where is your passport? Are you ready to meet the King of Kings? Is your name written in the Lamb's Book of Life? Have you complied with the disembarking instructions in Romans 10:9-13? Not one stowaway will be given entrance into the Kingdom of God!

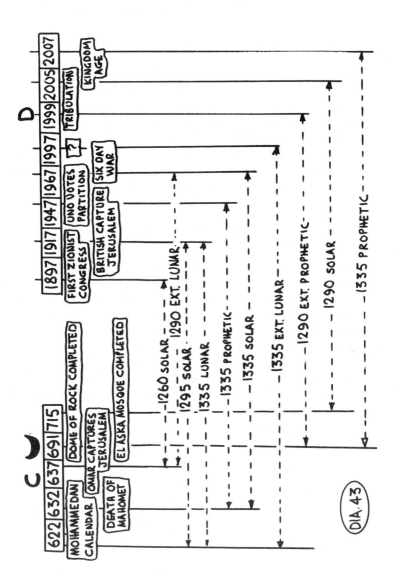

DIA. 43

Chapter Twelve

"A Time To Be Born, And A Time To Die"

"To everything there is a season, and a time to every PURPOSE under the heaven; a time to be BORN, and a time to DIE." (Ecclesiastes 3:1-2 NKJV)

"Man who is born of a woman .... his days are DETERMINED, the NUMBER of his months is with Thee, and his LIMITS Thou has set so that he cannot pass."

(Job 14:5)

These above verses are clearly demonstrated in the birth and death of Abraham and Isaac. We can discern a distinct pattern and a prophetic purpose in the determination of their days. We have seen repeatedly that timing with Isaac does not count with God until Ishmael was cast out and Isaac inherits in 1846 B.C. (See "Times of the Signs" p.110-114 and "The Sound of Music" chap.5).

If we plot on a chart the birth and death of Abraham, the year Isaac inherits and the year of his death, a perfect pattern stamped with the number seven becomes evident. (Dia. 44) Note on this diagram there are THREE (completeness, Godhead) time spans all multiples of SEVEN (perfection). The total span is 280 years which is 4 x 7 x 10 or spelling out the spiritual significance of these numbers we have - God's perfect (7) order (10) with His earthly (4) people.

We learn also that although Isaac lived to be 180 years old, in God's reckoning the first five years did not count whilst Ishmael was still living in Abraham's tents. With

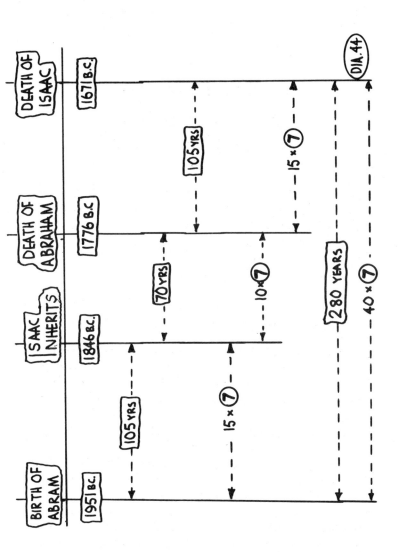

DIA. 44

God, Abraham and Isaac lived 175 years (5 x 5 x 7). What a waste are lives lived out of right relationship with God, e.g. the 38 years Israel wasted away in the wilderness (Deuteronomy 2:14).

"Only one life, 'twill soon be past,
Only what's done for Christ will last."

The Prophetic Pattern

The number SEVEN in the Bible is the great number of SPIRITUAL PERFECTION. In "Number in Scripture" (Bullinger) there are 42 pages detailing its wonders throughout the Bible. Dr. Ivan Panin also demonstrated the sevenfold pattern running through the numerical structure of the Bible. It also is vitally linked with chronophecy. Using the four key dates in the time spans of Abraham and Isaac as our starting points, we will find a startling, united, fourfold witness to key historic dates in Israel's history.

The Fall Of Jerusalem (Dia. 45)

"On the tenth day of the fifth month, in the nineteenth year of Nebuchadnezzar, King of Babylon, Nebuzaradan, Commander of the Imperial Guard, who served the King of Babylon, came to Jerusalem. He set fire to the TEMPLE OF THE LORD, the royal palace, and all the houses of Jerusalem. Every important building he burned down."

(Jeremiah 52:12-13 NIV)

The loss of their temple and capital city is one of the traumatic highlights in Jewish history; to this day they are still devastated by the memory of those tragic events in August and September 586 B.C.

Look at the amazing fourfold septenary pattern :-

1. From the birth of Abraham 1951 B.C. to 586 B.C. is 1365 years, i.e. 195 times SEVEN!

2. From the death of Abraham in 1776 B.C. to 586 B.C. is 1190 years, i.e. 170 times SEVEN!

3. From the year Isaac becomes the heir in 1846 B.C.

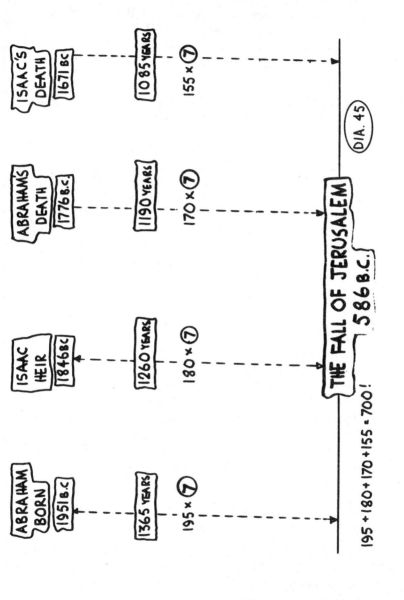

ABRAHAM BORN 1951 B.C · 1365 YEARS · 195 × ⑦

ISAAC HEIR 1846 B.C · 1260 YEARS · 180 × ⑦

ABRAHAM'S DEATH 1776 B.C · 1190 YEARS · 170 × ⑦

ISAAC'S DEATH 1671 B.C · 1085 YEARS · 155 × ⑦

THE FALL OF JERUSALEM 586 B.C.

195 + 180 + 170 + 155 = 700!

DIA. 45

until 586 B.C. is that great prophetic number 1260 years, i.e. 180 times SEVEN!

4. From the death of Isaac in 1671 B.C. to 586 B.C. is 1085 years, i.e. 155 times SEVEN!

If we add all these sevens we have 195 + 170 + 180 + 155 which equals exactly 700 times SEVEN!!

Jerusalem Again Becomes Israel's Capital (Dia. 46)

1949 A.D. is a critical prophetic year for Israel. In that year :-

(a) Israel moved its government to JERUSALEM, ignoring the U.N. vote to internationalize the city.

(b) Israel was admitted to the United Nations.

(c) Arab-Israeli war ends with Israel's victory over the Arab league.

(d) First elections in Israel; David Ben Gurion becomes Prime Minister.

(e) Jewish population of Israel reached the one million mark.

Again the marvellous fourfold septenary pattern unfolds :-

1. From the birth of Abraham 1951 B.C. to 1949 A.D. is 3899 years. i.e. 557 times SEVEN!

2. From the death of Abraham 1776 B.C. to 1949 A.D. is 3724 years, i.e. 532 times SEVEN!!

3. From the time Isaac inherits 1846 B.C. to 1949 A.D. is 3794 years, i.e. 542 times SEVEN!

4. From the death of Isaac 1671 B.C. to 1949 A.D. is 3619 years, i.e. 517 times SEVEN!

The Terminus Ad Quem - 2005 A.D. (Dia. 47)

How many times this year has cropped up in our historical and biblical bearings, the year power is delegated back to Israel, when the "Times of the Gentiles" will have run their course.

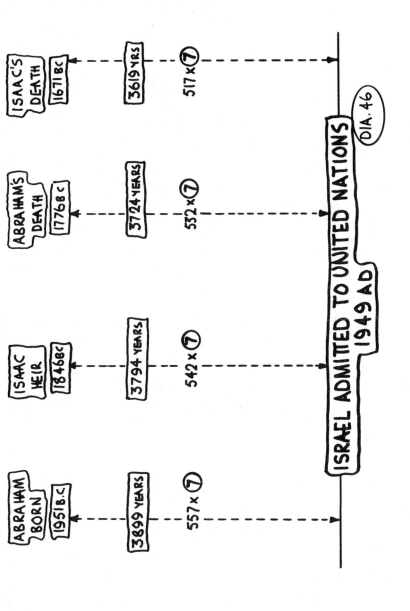

ABRAHAM BORN 1951 B.C.   3899 YEARS   557 × 7

ISAAC HEIR 1846 BC   3794 YEARS   542 × 7

ABRAHAM'S DEATH 1776 BC   3724 YEARS   532 × 7

ISAAC'S DEATH 1671 BC   3619 YRS   517 × 7

ISRAEL ADMITTED TO UNITED NATIONS 1949 AD

DIA. 46

155

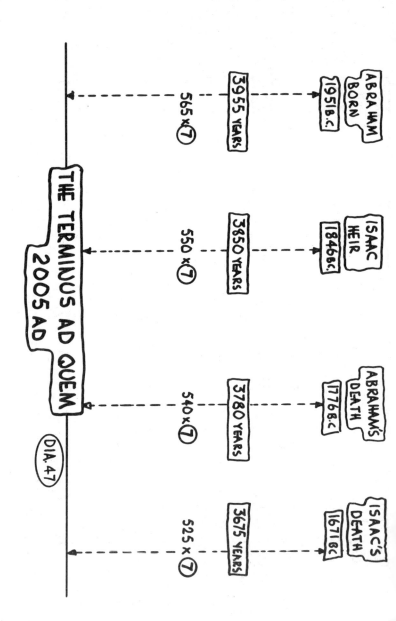

THE TERMINUS AD QUEM
2005 AD

DIA. 47

ABRAHAM BORN
1951 B.C.
3955 YEARS
565 x⑦

ISAAC HEIR
1846 B.C.
3850 YEARS
550 x⑦

ABRAHAM'S DEATH
1776 B.C.
3780 YEARS
540 x⑦

ISAAC'S DEATH
1671 B.C.
3675 YEARS
525 x⑦

Once again, the fourfold septenary pattern unfolds:-
1. From the birth of Abraham 1951 B.C. to 2005 A.D. is 3955 years, i.e. 565 times SEVEN!
2. From the death of Abraham 1776 B.C. to 2005 A.D. is 3780 years i.e. 540 times SEVEN!
3. From Isaac becoming the heir 1846 B.C. to 2005 A.D. is 3850 years, i.e. 550 times SEVEN!
4. From the death of Isaac in 1671 B.C. to 2005 A.D. is 3675 years, i.e. 525 times SEVEN!

Thus we find there are 2,180 SEVENS (565 + 540 + 550 + 525) all converging into 2005 A.D.!! SEVEN THE PERFECT NUMBER. Let's sing with Moses - *"I will proclaim the name of the Lord. Oh, praise the greatness of our God! He is the Rock, His works are PERFECT."* (Deuteronomy 32:3-4 NIV). David joins in the refrain - *"As for God, his way is perfect, the word of the Lord is flawless."* (2 Samuel 22:31 NIV)

As we see God's flawless timing from A to Z (Abraham to Zion 2005 A.D.), may we with renewed confidence *"Fix our eyes on JESUS, the author and perfector* (finisher) *of our faith."* (Hebrews 12:2 NIV)

Birth And Death of Jacob (Dia. 48)

Jacob (ISRAEL) is of course inextricably linked with Abraham and Isaac (Exodus 3:16, Deuteronomy 1:18, 2 Kings 13:23). We learn from his birth and death years, that there is a similar incredible septenary pattern joining up with key crisis years for Israel, viz:

1406 B.C. a) The crossing of Jordan and their entrance into Canaan.

135 A.D. b) The crushing of Bar Kochba's revolt, Judea depopulated and the Jews denationalized by the Romans.

1948 A.D. c) The rebirth of the State of Israel.

1997 A.D. d) See chap Nine '1997 in Chronophecy."

2004 A.D. e) If we work to exact decimal figures 1000 prophetic years = 985.6 years. Add two 1000 prophetic years 1971.2 and then add these to the Cross 33.25 A.D. we come to

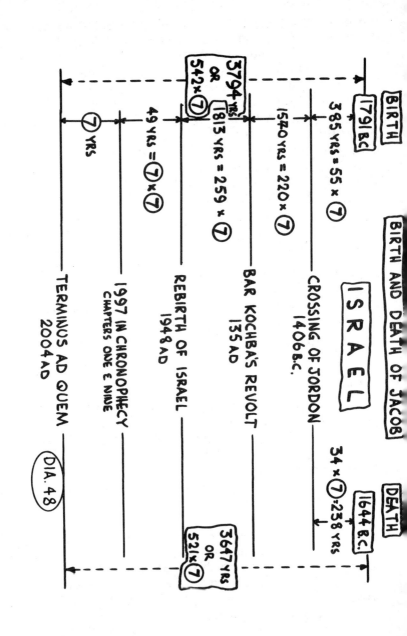

BIRTH AND DEATH OF JACOB

BIRTH
1791 B.C.

385 YRS = 55 × ⑦

1540 YRS = 220 × ⑦

CROSSING OF JORDON
1406 B.C.

ISRAEL

34 × ⑦ = 238 YRS

DEATH
1644 B.C.

BAR KOCHBA'S REVOLT
135 A.D.

1813 YRS = 259 × ⑦

3794 YRS
OR
542 × ⑦

REBIRTH OF ISRAEL
1948 A.D.

49 YRS = ⑦ × ⑦

1997 IN CHRONOPHECY
CHAPTERS ONE & NINE

⑦ YRS

TERMINUS AD QUEM
2004 A.D.

3647 YRS
OR
521 × ⑦

DIA. 48

158

2004.45 A.D.! A number of calculations come to 2004 plus so we have the terminus ad quem as 2004/2005 A.D. if we work closer than the nearest round number. Then all the restoration promises become a reality:-

"So do not fear, O Jacob my servant;
do not be dismayed, O Israel, declares the Lord.
I will surely save you out of a distant place,
your descendants from the land of their exile.
Jacob will again have security and peace,
and no one will make him afraid."(Jeremiah 30:10 NIV)

"Therefore it is what the Lord, who redeemed Abraham,
says to the house of Jacob:
No longer will Jacob be ashamed;
No longer will their faces grow pale.
When they see among their children,
the work of my hands,
they will keep my name holy;
they will acknowledge the holiness of the Holy One of Jacob,
and will stand in awe of the God of Israel."

(Isaiah 29:22-23 NIV)

Adam to 1997 A.D. (Dia. 49)

While on the subject of SEVENS if we convert some key solar years to prophetic years we will find a perfect pattern of SEVENS!

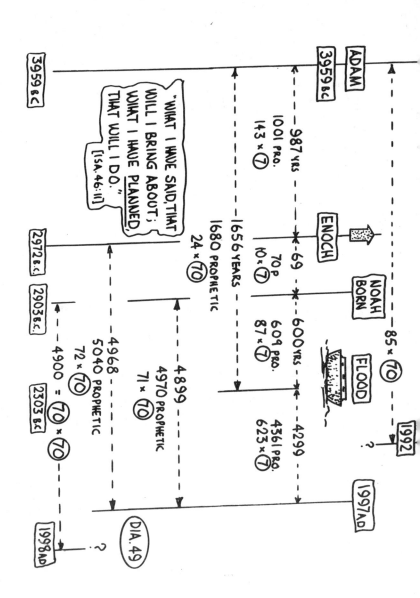

ADAM
3959 B.C.

3959 B.C.

987 YRS
1001 PRO.
143 × ⑦

"WHAT I HAVE SAID, THAT WILL I BRING ABOUT; WHAT I HAVE PLANNED, THAT WILL I DO."
[ISA. 46:11]

ENOCH

69
70 P.
10 × ⑦

NOAH BORN

1656 YEARS

1680 PROPHETIC
24 × ⑦

2972 B.C.

2903 B.C.

FLOOD

600 YRS
609 PRO.
87 × ⑦

4299

4361 PRO.
623 × ⑦

85 × ⑦

1992
?

4968
5040 PROPHETIC
72 × ⑦

4899
4970 PROPHETIC
71 × ⑦

4900 = ⑦ × ⑦

2303 B.C.

DIA.49

1997 A.D.

1998 A.D.
?

160

Chapter Thirteen

Chronophecy And The Genesis Genealogies
(back cover)

Do you remember in "1997 in Chronophecy" we quoted from Arthur Custance's striking statement:-

"I cannot believe that such detailed records from within a generation or two of Adam have been so perfectly preserved by accident. God has some purpose in mind: WE HAVE YET TO DISCOVER WHAT IT WAS."

Well in these genealogies there is a veritable prophetic goldmine. The key that unlocks the door in to this mine is found hanging up in Isaiah 46:10:-

"I make known the END from the BEGINNING, from ANCIENT TIMES what is STILL TO COME."

The most "ancient times" and the "beginning" are of course found in these genealogies in Genesis 5 and 11. How could they make known what is "STILL TO COME?" How could they make known the "END"? Having opened the door with this key, I entered this DARK and ancient goldmine, seeking to illuminate it with all the chronoprophetic light the Lord has so far graciously revealed to me through His Word. The first "golden" nugget I found was when I measured the time span from the death of Noah 1953 B.C. to 2007 A.D. - the beginning of the Millenial Age. Noah, in this sense, having survived the destruction of the "old world", was a type of those who would enter the Millenial Kingdom of rest. Noah's name in Hebrew means "REST". I did the simple calculation on my 'faithful "Sharp" calculator: 1953 + 2007 − 1 = 3959.

That number instantly rang a bell, because the creation of Adam was 3959 B.C.!! Was the "key" to these genealogies hanging up just inside the entrance to the mine? My chronoprophetic miner's lamp lit up Genesis 10:25 *"in the days of PELEG was the earth DIVIDED."* Was this another chronoprophetic clue? I added 3959 years to Peleg's death in 1963 B.C. (3959 − 1963 + 1) it came to 1997 A.D.! If this proves to be the year of the Rapture, the earth's people will be truly "divided" as millions of Christians are instantly translated (1 Thessalonians 4:17, 1 Corinthians 15:51-52). Peleg's name means "division" and the word "DIVIDE" and its derivatives refers to a channel or stream that divides the land. It is used of a stream of tears in Lamentations 3:48 - *"My eyes run down with streams of water, because of the destruction of the daughter of my people."* (NASB)

What a Niagra of tears will fall on this earth after the Rapture of the CHURCH!

Adam In Chronophecy

We read in Isaiah 46:10 - *"I make known the END from the BEGINNING."* Well the first recorded beginning in the Bible is the creation of Adam 3959 B.C. and his death 930 years later in 3029 B.C. So to any chrono-prophetically minded person, Adam must fairly bristle with end time dates! Wuest in his New Testament translation says:- *"Adam, who is a type of the one who is to come."* (Romans 5:14) So let us look more closely at his creation year 3959 B.C. 3959 equals 37 x 107! We learnt in chapter no. 7 "That Sublime Number" that 37 is the very special number of Jesus Christ. We learn in John 1:3 *"Through Him all things were made; without Him nothing was made that has been made."* (NIV). In Revelation 3:14 we read that Jesus Christ is *"the beginning of the creation of God"* so we see the number thirty-seven, the special SEAL of Jesus Christ stamped on the very year of Adam's creation. 37 and 107 are both PRIME numbers, i.e. they are not divisible by any other number e.g. 2, 3, 5, 7, 11, 13, 17, 19 etc. Now 37 is the twelfth prime number. Bullinger says:- "Twelve is a perfect number signifying perfection of government." Darby says:- "twelve is the number always used to indicate POWER, the power of God's administration among men."

107 is the 28th PRIME NUMBER, i.e. 4 x 7, so combining the two prime numbers of 3959 – 37 x 107 - the 12th and 28th, we have "God's administrative power (12) perfectly (7) demonstrated on earth" (4).

If we measure from 3959 B.C. to our first End Time date 1999 A.D. we have a time span of (3959 + 1999 – 1) 5957 years which is stamped with the royal insignia of Jesus Christ - 161 times THIRTY-SEVEN!

Measuring from his DEATH in 3029 B.C. to 2004 A.D. yields 5032 years which is linked with two very special numbers 37 and 17 (see the "S" Factor) because:-

136 x 137 and 296 x 17 both equal 5032 years!! Surely, *"he being DEAD yet speaketh"* (Hebrews 11:4).

If we measure to 2005 A.D. from his death 3029 B.C. we have 5033 years which is 719 x SEVEN! That perfect number again.

Seth (Genesis 5:3-8)

Seth's death speaks loud and clear of the END. From his death in 2917 B.C. to 2005 A.D. is 4921 years which is 133 times THIRTY-SEVEN, the Royal Insignia, or 703 times SEVEN, the perfect number!

From his birth 3829 B.C. to 2003 A.D. is 5831 years; which is 343 times SEVENTEEN, the salvation number; or 833 times SEVEN, the perfect number!

Seth means "appointed" or "set". It reminds me of a verse in Daniel 8:12, *"I am going to tell you what will happen in the TIME OF WRATH ... the appointed time of the end."* (NKJV). Surely 2003 A.D. will be right in the midst of the time of God's outpoured wrath (Revelation 6:16, 6:17, 11:18, 14:10, 14:19, 15:1, 15:7, 16:1, 16:19, 19:15).

Lamech (Genesis 5:25-31)

Lamech, the father of Noah, said at his son's birth, *"He will comfort us in the labour and painful toil of our hands caused by the ground the Lord has cursed."* (v. 29 NIV).One commentator on these words says:- "Lamech's words are to be understood as pointing forward to a new beginning which would bring nearer the final act of God by which the curse would be lifted from the earth - Noah means REST - the rest signified in his name shall be produced by a consolation coming through the work of judgment in his time." (Genesis H.G. Stigers)

Lamech's history is riddled with the perfect number seven, *"when Lamech had lived 182 years, he had a son"* 182 = 26 x 7 *"after Noah was born, Lamech lived 595 years"* 595 = 85 x 7 *"altogether Lamech lived 777 years"*. 777 = 111 x 7, 777 also equals 21 x 37 or 3 x 7 x 37, the royal insignia of Jesus Christ!

Lamech lived just prior to the great flood judgment, so he should be a chronoprophetic clue to the greater Tribulation judgment of 1999 - 2005 A.D. Remember *"I make known from ANCIENT TIMES what is STILL TO COME"* (Isaiah 46:10). He was born in 3085 B.C. and the time span to 1999 A.D. is 5083 years which equals 299 x SEVENTEEN!

"In the six hundredth year of Noah's life, on the SEVENTEENTH day of the second month - on THAT DAY all the springs of the great deep burst forth, and the floodgates of the heavens were opened. And rain fell on the earth forty days and forty nights" (Genesis 7:11-12 NIV). 299 equals 13 x 23. THIRTEEN occurs first in Genesis 14:4, *"Twelve years they served Chedorlaomer, and in the THIRTEENTH year they rebelled."*

"Every occurrence of the number thirteen, and likewise of every multiple of it, stamps that which it stands in connection with rebellion, apostasy, defection, corruption, disintegration, revolution or some kindred idea." (Number in Scripture p. 203 Bullinger).

The multiple of thirteen in this connection is 23 which

is the NINTH prime number, the number above all others connected with judgement - 2, 3, 5, 7, 11, 13, 17, 19, 23!

Lamech's chronophecy certainly anticipates coming judgment before the Millenial rest. We drew attention earlier to the emphasis on the number SEVEN in Lamech's life. This is a good chronoprophetic clue. From his birth in 3085 B.C. to 2005 A.D. is a time span of 5085 years which is 727 times SEVEN! From his death in 2308 B.C. to 2005 A.D. is 4312 years which is 616 times SEVEN!

Lamech's name means "to bring low"; five years after his death God's devastating deluge brought low *"the heroes of old, men of renown"* (Genesis 6:4). No material progress of men, nor their renown could prevent the hour of retribution. Likewise during the Tribulation, *"so shall it be at the end of the age. The Son of Man shall send forth his angels, and they shall gather out of His kingdom all things that offend, and them that do iniquity"* (Matthew 13:40-41).

"The Kingdom of God begins with a garbage can, with the angels as the garbage collectors ... the eschatological wrath of God is the bulldozer to clear the ground of slum political and social systems. Its purpose is to demolish the economic rat-traps in which two thirds of mankind are caught and kept in poverty. Above all, man's military organisations must be destroyed so that nations shall not learn war any more." (Christ's Return to Rule the World. A. Longley p.48).

These early genealogies certainly make *"known the END"* and *"what is still to COME"*. I have gone deeply into every name listed and it's a marvellous study, but I feel that to repeat it all in one reading, it could become tedious and give you chronoprophetic indigestion! I hope I have given you enough clues to encourage you to search out a few "golden" nuggets for yourself.

Chapter Fourteen

The Overall Symmetry of Redemptive Chronology (Dia. 49A)

We have seen in previous chapters the perfect symmetry of history from the Babylonian era until the end (2005 A.D.) and now we are to learn the perfect symmetry of ALL history as related to God's redemptive purposes. Let us see His perfect sovereign control from A to Z (Adam to Zion).

STEP 1 BIRTH OF ADAM

In the ninth chapter we pointed out how the year 3959 B.C. is the terminus a quo of redemptive chronology for the creation of ADAM. There we found a discrepancy of 45 years from Ussher's date of 4004 B.C. Doing further research we found that Ussher dates the DIVISION of Israel into the ten tribes as 975 B.C. whereas Edwin Thiele in his brilliant book, "The Mysterious Numbers of the Hebrew Kings" gives us the year 930 B.C. (3rd Edition p.79). The difference between 975 and 930 B.C. being of course 45 years! Thus Ussher's dating of Adam in 4004 B.C. is exactly 45 years too early. When we work confidently from the Bible text of 3959 B.C. as the birth of redemptive chronology, an amazing pattern unfolds. If we tally up the time spans in Genesis chapters 5 and 11, we discover there is exactly 2008 years from Adam to the birth of Abram (later renamed Abraham) in 1951 B.C.

THE PERFECT SYMMETRY OF REDEMPTIVE HISTORY

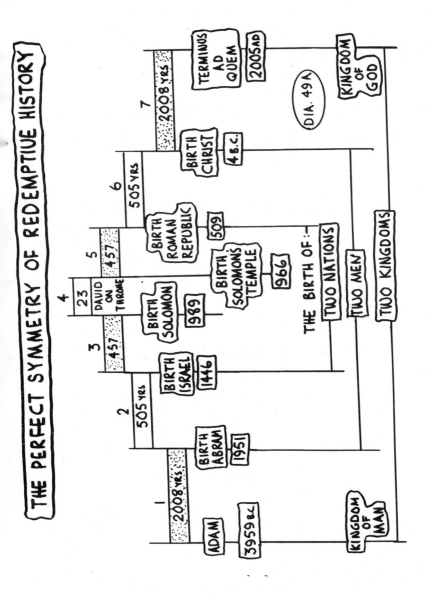

STEP 2 BIRTH OF JEWISH NATION

From the birth of Abraham in 1951 B.C. it is exactly 505 years until the birth of a fully fledged nation Israel at the Exodus 1446 B.C. (Exodus 12). Incidentally, from 1951 B.C. until the fall of Jerusalem in 70 A.D. is 2020 years or 4 times 505! Wheels within wheels.

STEP 3 BIRTH OF SOLOMON

From the birth of Israel as a nation 1446 B.C. until the birth of Solomon 989 B.C. is 457 years. (Bedford - refer Bibliography).

STEP 4 BIRTH OF SOLOMON'S TEMPLE

From the birth of Solomon 989 B.C. until the building of the Temple in 966 B.C. is 23 years. This is the central span; if we bisect it, we have 977 B.C. when David had been on the throne for 33 years, and it represents the peak period of Hebrew prosperity under the monarchy.

STEP 5 BIRTH OF ROMAN REPUBLIC

This step in its symmetry matches Step 3 with a time interval of 457 years, bringing us from the temple start 966 B.C. to 509 B.C. All history books are unanimous that 509 B.C. was the start of the Roman Republic. "During the period of the Republic Rome extended its boundaries at first over all Italy, and finally over the whole Mediterranean world." (Westminster Dictionary of the Bible p.810)

Rome figures very prominently in Jewish history. Christ was born into the Roman Empire. It was Roman soldiers who crucified the Lord of Glory. It was the Roman army that sacked Jerusalem, destroyed the Temple and dispersed the Jewish nation worldwide (70-135 A.D.). Antichrist will be a Roman prince *"and the people* (Romans) *of the prince WHO IS TO COME* (yet future) *will destroy the city and the sanctuary"* 70 A.D. (Daniel 9:26) Refer Appendix 2, "Times of the Signs."

As Rome is so integrally intertwined with Jerusalem both in history and prophecy, we are not surprised that the birth of the Republic of Rome is included in the overall symmetry of redemptive chronology.

STEP 6 BIRTH OF CHRIST

Matching Step 2 we extend 505 years on from the birth of the Republic of Rome in 509 B.C. and we come to the year 4 B.C. for the birth of Christ!

"Civilised time is dated from the birth of Jesus Christ. The centuries carry this signature, and the years of our modern world are labelled by common consent the 'years of our Lord'....

Only one EVENT towers high enough above the horizon of history to serve as a landmark and a time measure for all civilised races. Faith, of course, sees in that deep mark on human almanacs a mysterious and, as far as human purpose is concerned, an undesigned, but all-significant, token of ownership. It corresponds to the stamp on the coin. It answers the challenge, 'whose image and superscription is this?' It is both a sign and a prophecy; a sign that the centuries belong to Christ, a prophecy of the fast-coming hour when all that TIME includes and represents shall bear this signature." (The Unrealized Logic of Religion, p.23 W.H. Fitchett).

Later in this chapter we will see the significance of 4 B.C. in the light of Galatians 4:4, *"when the fulness of TIME was come, God sent forth His Son, made of a woman, in order that He might REDEEM."*

STEP 7 THE BIRTH OF THE NEW AGE

Matching Step One we extend 2008 years from 4 B.C. and we come once more to that most significant year 2005 A.D.! The terminal date of man's control of planet

169

earth, the end of the 70th week of Daniel, and the beginning of the glorious Kingdom of God, with Christ reigning from Jerusalem.

THE FULNESS OF TIME

"But when the FULNESS OF TIME (CHRONOS) was come, God sent forth His Son, made of a woman, made under the law to REDEEM those who were under the law."

(Galatians 4:4 NKJV)

Later in Ephesians 1:10 we read of a different word translated 'TIMES':-

"That in the dispensation of the fulness of TIMES (KAIROS) He might gather together in one all things in Christ, both which are in Heaven, and which are on earth, even in HIM."

The word 'Kairos' refers to periods, time spans, seasons, often with intervals between the durations of time. Note it is in the plural "fulness of TIMES."

But in Galatians it is a different word and in the singular, "the fulness of TIME." This is the Greek word chronos from which we derive our word 'chronology' and it refers to 'successive years' not just a segment of time. (Refer to Dia.70 p.208 in 'Times of the Signs').

As it deals with continuous years we can confidently measure the time span from Adam to Christ, expecting to learn the nature of its 'fulness.' As has often been pointed out it was:-

The fulness of time POLITICALLY.

The civilised world had been united by three facts - Roman peace, Roman roads and a common language - Greek.

The fulness of time SOCIALLY

It was an age of anxiety and despair.

The fulness of time RELIGIOUSLY.

There was a sense of crisis, the Jews were expectant and waiting but it is also in strict context of:-

The fulness of time CHRONOLOGICALLY.

From Adam (3959 B.C.) to the birth of Christ (4 B.C.) is a time span of 3955 solar years. What is the spiritual significance of 3955? Reduced to its prime numbers we have 113 x 7 x 5 = 3955.

    113 is the 30TH PRIME NUMBER)   SEE
      7 is the 4TH PRIME NUMBER) APPENDIX
      5 is the 3RD PRIME NUMBER)   TWO

In Bullinger's book "Number in Scripture" he states:-

"30 being 3 x 10 denotes in a higher degree the perfection of Divine Order, as marking the RIGHT MOMENT. Christ was 30 years of age at the commencement of His ministry, Luke 3:23" p. 265. See also Joseph - Genesis 41:46; David - 2 Samuel 5:4; Priests - Numbers 4:23.

4 is the great WORLD NUMBER of mankind made up of *"lands, tongues, families, nations."* (Genesis 10:5, 20, 21). It comprises all that God loved when He sent His Son, *"God so loved the WORLD ..."* (John 3:16).

3, therefore, stands for that which is solid, real, substantial, COMPLETE & ENTIRE. All things that are specially COMPLETE are stamped with the number three." (Bullinger p.107)

Putting these three numbers together we can see how they truly represent "the FULNESS of TIME" when Christ was made flesh and dwelt among us.

At exactly the right moment (30) in history, the incarnate Son of God came to the family of mankind (4) when the complete, entire number of years (3) were fulfilled! .

Prophetic Years

If we convert these 3955 solar years from Adam to Christ into prophetic years, we come up with 3955 x (365.2421 ÷ 360) or 3955 x 1.045 = 4012 prophetic years.

Do you remember in Chapter 4 "The 'S' Factor" we learnt about the number seventeen, and how it ran all the way through Judah's history from their deportation in 597 B.C. to 2005 A.D. (153 x 17 years)? We saw how the number 17 means:-

"God has sworn on oath that the COMPLETE cycle of events He has ordered will be perfectly accomplished."

Would it not be wonderful if this sweet number cropped up in the "FULNESS of TIME"?

Well, as we have seen from Adam to the birth of Christ is 4012 prophetic years (i.e. 360 days to a year). How thrilled I was when I tapped 4012 onto my pocket calculator and then divided by 17, pressing the equals sign. Up came the number 236 - yes, 4012 is perfectly divisible by 17 - the number of COMPLETE cycles!

What about 236, are there any seventeens lurking in this number? I divided it by seventeen, up came 13.88 on the screen. No the answer was not on the surface. So I factorized it to find the prime numbers, they are 2 x 2 x 59 - I turned to my prime numbers chart (appendix 2) could it be possible? - Here are the first seventeen prime numbers - 2, 3, 5, 7, 11, 13, 17, 19, 23, 29, 31, 37, 41, 43, 47, 53 and (59). Praise the Lord, 59 is the SEVENTEENTH prime number!

Chapter Fifteen

Conclusion

The words of Dr. Grattan Guiness written last century in "Light for the Last Days" form a fitting conclusion to my two books on Chronophecy:

"We venture to assert that those who take the trouble to follow the investigations of chronology, Bible in hand, will not fail to be at the close more profoundly convinced than ever before of the inspiration of the sacred volume, of the all embracing providence and foreknowledge of God, and of the near approach of the end of this age. We would earnestly request that our readers verify the chronological calculations for themselves. They must indeed do this in order to have any firm, well-grounded conviction on the subject. Merely to read a number of statements as to events, dates, and intervals produces but an evanescent impression on the mind. Our desire is that even students of the subject should be able to say with the men of Samaria, "Now we believe, not because of your saying"; for we have studied for ourselves, and know that this is indeed the truth.

The events should be considered, whether they are indeed as critical and important, in connection with the historical movements to which they respectively belong, as we represent them to be. The dates should be verified where needful, and above all the calculations on which our conclusions rest. (The simple operation of addition and subtraction are alone required for this.) It is one thing to receive a dogmatic statement, and quite another to investigate the facts for oneself.

We would wish our readers to share the feelings of surprise, of awe, and of adoration which we ourselves have experienced, when earnest prayer, patient, reverent searching of the Scriptures, and study of "books", have from time to time been rewarded by the opening of the eyes to see, one after another, the facts which form links in a chain of evidence, which demonstrates the system of prophetic chronology.

Only gradually and one by one did they come to our knowledge; many a calculation made revealed nothing, but we believed that a Divine order pervaded the times of history and prophecy, as it pervades all the other works and ways of God. We know that appearances were not to be trusted, that the seemingly lawless and erratic movements of planets and comets are in reality regulated by the most exact laws, that the countless anomalies of nature are all capable of classification, and exhibit perfect and wonderful order. We had no doubt that it was the same with these sacred "times", and hence we continued our search, till all became, step by step, clear. And now we invite other Christian students critically to examine the results here presented; for if they are true, every Christian ought to know it, every preacher ought to proclaim it, the world ought to be warned of its fast approaching doom, and the Church ought to be cheered by the assurance of the nearness of her "blessed hope".

("Light for the Last Days" pp 220-222)

Appendix No. 1

God's Prophetic Time Scales (Dia. 50)

There are three scales used in the Bible for measuring the TIME between two historic events:

1. SOLAR TIME or calendar time 365.24 days to a year.
2. PROPHETIC TIME 360 days a year.
3. LUNAR TIME The earth, sun and moon are in a straight line every 29.53 days and twelve of these months equals 12 x 29.53 = 354.36 days to a year. The Mohammedan calendar uses a lunar year - and year one on the Moslem calendar started on the 13th September 622 A.D.

These three scales bear a relation to one another known as reduced or extended ratios. For example, in the "Symmetry of the Temples" from 624 B.C. to 2005 A.D. is 2628 years. If we reduce this span by the prophetic ratio we have 2628 x 360 ÷ 365.24 = 2590 solar years. Measuring 2590 years from 624 B.C. brings us to 1967 A.D. (the Six Day War).

Now on the chart we have the normal solar years found in Bible measurements. On the left-hand-side we have this normal scale **reduced** into lunar and prophetic years e.g.

1260 x 354.36 ÷ 365.24 = 1222.46 LUNAR YEARS

1260 x 360 ÷ 365.24 = 1241.92 PROPHETIC YEARS

On the right-hand-side we have 1260 solar years **extended:-**

1260 x 365.24 ÷ 354.36 = 1298.68 LUNAR YEARS

1260 x 365.24 ÷ 360 = 1278.34 PROPHETIC YEARS

and so on down the scale.

GOD'S PROPHETIC TIME SCALES

APPENDIX NO.

	REDUCED	NORMAL	EXTENDED	REFERENCE
	1222.46 LUNAR 1241.92 PROPHETIC	1260 SOLAR	1298.68 LUNAR 1278.34 PROPHETIC	REV.11:3 etc.
	2444.93 L 2483.84 P	2520 s	2597.37 L 2556.68 P	TWICE 1260
	1251.57 L 1271.49 P	1290 s	1329.60 L 1308.77 P	DAN.12:11
	2503.14 L 2542.98 P	2580 s	2659.21 L 2617.55 P	TWICE 1290
	1295.23 L 1315.84 P	1335 s	1375.98 L 1354.43 P	DAN.12:12
	2590.46 L 2631.69 P	2670 s	2751.97 L 2708.86 P	TWICE 1335
	1256.42 L 1276.42 P	1295 s	1334.76 L 1313.84 P	HALF 2590
	2512.84 L 2552.84 P	2590 s	2669.52 L 2627.69 P	1260+1260+70
	1867.65 L 1897.38 P	1925 s	1984.10 L 1953.01 P	HALF 3850
	3735.31 L 3794.76 P	3850 s	3968.20 L 3906.03 P	1260+70+ 2520
	PROPHETIC YEAR 360 DAYS	SOLAR YEAR 365.2421 DAYS	LUNAR YEAR 354.36 DAYS	

Another example can be seen in the "Symmetry of the times of the Temples" - from 70 A.D. (sacking of Jerusalem) to 1312 A.D. (Knight Templars abolished) is 1242 solar years. Now 1242 solar years equal 1260 prophetic years (1242 x 365.24 ÷ 360 = 1260).

Appendix No. 2

Prime Numbers

2	3	5	7	11	13	17	19	23	29	31	37	41
43	47	53	59	61	67	71	73	79	83	89	97	101
103	107	109	113	127	131	137	139	149	151	157	163	167
173	179	181	191	193	197	199	211	223	227	229	233	239
241	251	257	263	269	271	277	281	283	293	307	311	313
317	331	337	347	349	353	359	367	373	379	383	389	397
401	409	419	421	431	433	439	443	449	457	461	463	467
479	487	491	499	503	509	521	523	541	547	557	563	569
571	577	587	593	599	601	607	613	617	619	631	641	643
647	653	659	661	673	677	683	691	701	709	719	727	733
739	743	751	757	761	769	773	787	797	809	811	821	823
827	829	839	853	857	859	863	877	881	883	887	907	911
919	929	937	941	947	953	967	971	977	983	991	997	1009
1013	1019	1021	1031	1033	1039	1049	1051	1061	1063	1069	1087	1091
1093	1097	1103	1109	1117	1123	1129	1151	1153	1163	1171	1181	1187
1193	1201	1213	1217	1223	1229	1231	1237	1249	1259	1277	1279	1283
1289	1291	1297	1301	1303	1307	1319	1321	1327	1361	1367	1373	1381
1399	1409	1423	1427	1429	1433	1439	1447	1451	1453	1459	1471	1481
1483	1487	1489	1493	1499	1511	1523	1531	1543	1549	1553	1559	1567
1571	1579	1583	1597	1601	1607	1609	1613	1619	1621	1627	1637	1657
1663	1667	1669	1693	1697	1699	1709	1721	1723	1733	1741	1747	1753
1759	1777	1783	1787	1789	1801	1811	1823	1831	1847	1861	1867	1871
1873	1877	1879	1889	1901	1907	1913	1931	1933	1949	1951	1973	1979
1987	1993	1997	1999	2003	2011	2017	2027	2029	2039	2053	2063	2069
2081	2083	2087	2089	2099	2111	2113	2129	2131	2137	2131	2143	2153
2161	2179	2203	2207	2213	2221	2237	2239	2243	2251	2267	2269	2273
2281	2287	2293	2297	2309	2311	2333	2339	2341	2347	2351	2357	2371
2377	2381	2383	2389	2393	2399	2411	2417	2423	2437	2441	2447	2459
2467	2473	2477	2503	2521	2531	2539	2543	2549	2551	2557	2579	2591
2593	2609	2617	2621	2633	2647	2657	2659	2663	2671	2677	2683	2687
2689	2693	2699	2707	2711	2713	2719	2729	2731	2741	2749	2753	2767
2777	2789	2791	2797	2801	2803	2819	2833	2837	2843	2851	2857	2861
2879	2887	2897	2903	2909	2917	2927	2939	2953	2957	2963	2969	2971
2999	3001	3011	3019	3023	3037	3041	3049	3061	3067	3079	3083	3089
3109	3119	3121	3137	3163	3167	3169	3181	3187	3191	3203	3209	3217
3221	3229	3251	3253	3257	3259	3271	3299	3301	3307	3313	3319	3323
3329	3331	3343	3347	3359	3361	3371	3373	3389	3391	3407	3413	3433
3449	3457	3461	3463	3467	3469	3491	3499	3511	3517	3527	3529	3533
3539	3541	3547	3557	3559	3571	3581	3583	3593	3607	3613	3617	3623
3631	3637	3643	3659	3671	3673	3677	3691	3697	3701	3709	3719	3727
3733	3739	3761	3767	3769	3779	3793	3797	3803	3821	3823	3833	3847
3851	3853	3863	3877	3881	3889	3907	3911	3917	3919	3923	3929	3931
3943	3947	3967	3989	4001	4003	4007	4013	4019	4021	4027	4049	4051
4057	4073	4079	4091	4093	4099	4111	4127	4129	4133	4139	4153	4157
4159	4177	4201	4211	4217	4219	4229	4231	4241	4243	4253	4259	4261
4271	4273	4283	4289	4297	4327	4337	4339	4349	4357	4363	4373	4391
4397	4409	4421	4423	4441	4447	4451	4457	4463	4481	4483	4493	4507

4513	4517	4519	4523	4547	4549	4561	4567	4583	4591	4597	4603	4621
4637	4639	4643	4649	4651	4657	4663	4673	4679	4691	4703	4721	4723
4729	4733	4751	4759	4783	4787	4789	4793	4799	4801	4813	4817	4831
4861	4871	4877	4889	4903	4909	4919	4931	4933	4937	4943	4951	4957
4967	4969	4973	4987	4993	4999	5003	5009	5011	5021	5023	5039	5051
5059	5077	5081	5087	5099	5101	5107	5113	5119	5147	5153	5167	5171
5179	5189	5197	5209	5227	5231	5233	5237	5261	5273	5279	5281	5297
5303	5309	5323	5333	5347	5351	5381	5387	5393	5399	5407	5413	5417
5419	5431	5437	5441	5443	5449	5471	5477	5479	5483	5501	5503	5507
5519	5521	5527	5531	5557	5563	5569	5573	5581	5591	5623	5639	5641
5647	5651	5653	5657	5659	5669	5683	5689	5693	5701	5711	5717	5737
5741	5743	5749	5779	5783	5791	5801	5807	5813	5821	5827	5839	5843
5849	5851	5857	5861	5867	5869	5879	5881	5897	5903	5923	5927	5939
5953	5981	5987	6007	6011	6029	6037	6043	6047	6053	6067	6073	6079
6089	6091	6101	6113	6121	6131	6133	6143	6151	6163	6173	6197	6199
6203	6211	6217	6221	6229	6247	6257	6263	6269	6271	6277	6287	6299
6301	6311	6317	6323	6329	6337	6343	6353	6359	6361	6367	6373	6379
6389	6397	6421	6427	6449	6451	6469	6473	6481	6491	6521	6529	6547
6551	6553	6563	6569	6571	6577	6581	6599	6607	6619	6637	6653	6659
6661	6673	6679	6689	6691	6701	6703	6709	6719	6733	6737	6761	6763
6779	6781	6791	6793	6803	6823	6827	6829	6833	6841	6857	6863	6869
6871	6883	6899	6907	6911	6917	6947	6949	6959	6961	6967	6971	6977
6983	6991	6997	7001	7013	7019	7027	7039	7043	7057	7069	7079	7103
7109	7121	7127	7129	7151	7159	7177	7187	7193	7207	7211	7213	7219
7229	7237	7243	7247	7253	7283	7297	7307	7309	7321	7331	7333	7349
7351	7369	7393	7411	7417	7433	7451	7457	7459	7477	7481	7487	7489
7499	7507	7517	7523	7529	7537	7541	7547	7549	7559	7561	7573	7577
7583	7589	7591	7603	7607	7621	7639	7643	7649	7669	7673	7681	7687
7691	7699	7703	7717	7723	7727	7741	7753	7757	7759	7789	7793	7817
7823	7829	7841	7853	7867	7873	7877	7879	7883	7901	7907	7919	7927
7933	7937	7949	7951	7963	7993	8009	8011	8017	8039	8053	8059	8069
8081	8087	8089	8093	8101	8111	8117	8123	8147	8161	8167	8171	8179
8191	8209	8219	8221	8231	8233	8237	8243	8263	8629	8273	8287	8291

Appendix No. 3
The Genealogies from Adam to Joseph
Inside back cover

Appendix No. 4
Comparison Of Chronological Systems

We have included at this stage three charts from John Walton's "Chronological and background charts of the Old Testament" (Zondervan).

The system that has been used in my two books is EARLY EXODUS 1446 B.C. and SHORT SOJOURN in Egypt (215 yrs). This lines up perfectly with the Bible text and chronophecy. The reference to 430 years in Egypt in Exodus 12:40 is made clearer in the LXX and the Samaritan text which read "the sojourning of the children of Israel who sojourned in Egypt and in the land of Canaan was 430 years."

Ussher, Anstey, Bedford etc. all give 215 years for Israel's sojourn in Egypt. For a clear explanation see "Chronology of the Old Testament" Anstey (pages 64-66).

Comparison of Chronological Systems

EARLY EXODUS LONG SOJOURN	EARLY EXODUS SHORT SOJOURN		LATE EXODUS	RECONSTRUCTIONIST
The Patriarchs 2166-1805		21|00		
Migration to Egypt 1876		20|00		
		19|00		
	The Patriarchs 1952-1589	18|00	The Patriarchs 1950-1650	
Egyptian Sojourn 1876-1446	Migration to Egypt 1660	17|00	Migration to Egypt 1650	
		16|00		
Slavery 1730 or 1580	Egyptian Sojourn 1660-1446 Slavery: 1580	15|00	Egyptian Sojourn 1650-1230	The Patriarchs 1500-1300 Gradual migration
Wandering 1446-1406	Wandering: 1446-1406	14|00	Slavery: 1580	Egyptian Sojourn 1350-1230
Conquest and Judges 1406-1050	Conquest and Judges 1406-1050	13|00		
		12|00	Conquest and Judges 1230-1025	Conquest and Judges 1230-1025
		11|00		
United Kingdom 1050-931	United Kingdom 1050-931	10|00	United Kingdom 1025-931	United Kingdom 1025-931
		9|00		
Early date for Exodus and 430-year sojourn in Egypt per Masoretic reading of Exod. 12:40	Early date of Exodus and 215-year sojourn in Egypt per LXX reading of Exod. 12:40		Late date of Exodus and belief in historicity of patriarchal events	Late date of Exodus and reconstruction of biblical history through use of form criticism
L. Wood, J. Davis, Unger, and G. Archer	J. Free and S. Schultz		R. K. Harrison, G. E. Wright, K. A. Kitchen, and W. F. Albright	A. Alt, M. Noth, C. Gordon, and H. H. Rowley

authors named may vary as to the exact dates, but they fall generally in the given school of thought.

Date of the Exodus:
Part I

15th-CENTURY EVIDENCE	13th-CENTURY REBUTTAL
I Kings 6:1 designates 480 years from the Exodus to Solomon's dedication of the Temple. The dedication was 966. That makes the Exodus 1446.	The 480 years is most likely 12 generations (12x40=480). In actuality a generation was about 25 years, making the actual figure about 300.
The "Dream Stela" of Thutmose IV on the sphinx gives evidence that Thutmose was not legal heir to the throne. Would be logical that eldest son was killed in the 10th plague.	Only one of many other possibilities. No proof that the Biblical plague was involved in the death of the rightful he
In Judges 11:26, Jephthah assigns 300 years between his day (c. 1100) and the Conquest. This would seem to indicate a 15th-century Exodus.	This was a generalization or a rough and slightly inaccurate guess by Jephthah who would have had no access to historical records.
To support the biblical chronology of Moses, Pharaoh must have reigned in excess of 40 years. Moses stayed in the wilderness until Pharaoh died. Only possibilities: Thutmose III, Rameses II.	Moses' 40 years with the Midianites is not really a chronological reference
The Last Level at Hazor, wiped out by Barak and Deborah, contains Mycenaean IIIB Pottery; this requires, at the latest, a date in the late 13th century. This pushes Exodus much earlier.	The judges overlapped enough to accommodate this.
The Merneptah Stela (c. 1220) mentions Israel by name. They must have been there for a long time for the Egyptians to accept them as a nation.	Fifty years would have been sufficient time.
The Amarna Tablets (1400) tell of the upheaval caused by the "Habiru." This could have been the Hebrews, possibly classified under a general category.	The "Habiru" can in no way be identified with the Israelites.
The length of time assigned to the judges period in Scripture, even with overlapping, cannot be squeezed into the century and a half allowed by a 13th-century Exodus.	With overlaps and understanding of th symbolic nature of time spans, it can b fitted in.

Date of the Exodus:
Part II

13th-CENTURY EVIDENCE	15th-CENTURY REBUTTAL
The civilizations of Edom, Moab, and Ammon were not in existence in the 15th century. Since Israel had contact with them, the Exodus must be later.	Finds at the Timna Temple indicate sedentary civilizations in Negev at least in early 14th century. Tribes were wandering earlier than that.
The destruction of Lachish, Debir, and Bethel were in the 13th century, as indicated by the layer of ash.	Lachish, Debir, and Bethel are not said to have been burned at the time of the Conquest. The layer of ash could be due to Egypt's conquests.
In Exodus 1:11, Israelites were said to have been building the city of Rameses. This must be in honor of Rameses II of 13th century.	(1) Name "Rameses" used much earlier than 13th century. (2) City was being built before birth of Moses; thus, before Rameses II, even with late Exodus. (3) This was a store city, not a capital.
The 430 years of Exodus 12:40 cannot fit in with the Hyksos period.	The Hebrews need not be related to the Hyksos. There is much evidence that Jacob went to Egypt almost 150 years before the Hyksos period began.
Thutmose III was not known as a great builder and therefore does not fit into the historical picture.	Though not known as a great builder, Thutmose III is known to have had some building projects in the delta region.
Scripture does not mention the Palestinian invasions of Seti I or Rameses II. Therefore, Exodus must have been in 13th century and Israel was not yet in Palestine.	It is very likely that the periods of "rest" during the Judges were the periods of tighter Egyptian control. The Egyptian invasions were against the Canaanites.
Pushing the Exodus back means pushing the Patriarchs back, and the Patriarchs cannot go back any farther.	There is just as much evidence for putting the Patriarchs in Middle Bronze I as there is for putting them in Middle Bronze II.

Appendix No. 5
Calculating B.C. to A.D.

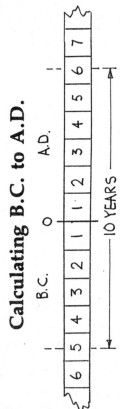

RULE ONE
B.C. 5 + 10 YRS. = A.D. 6

SUBTRACT YEARS TO BE ADDED TO THE B.C. FIGURE, THEN ADD ONE YEAR.

$$10 - 5 = 5 + 1 = 6 A.D.$$

RULE TWO
A.D. 6 - 10 YRS = B.C. 5

SUBTRACT, THEN ADD ONE YEAR.

$$10 - 6 = 4 + 1 = 5 B.C.$$

RULE THREE
B.C. 5 TO A.D. 6 = 10 YRS.

ADD B.C. YEARS TO A.D. YEARS, THEN SUBTRACT ONE.

$$B.C. 5 + A.D. 6 = 11 - 1 = 10 YRS.$$

DIA 52

Appendix No. 6
Waypoint No. 6

In "Times of the Signs" (p.95) we pointed out that 1988 would see a key development in Israel's history. From Diagram No. 53 we can see that our measuring rod has the choice of three different years for its terminus a quo; this is because of the Babylonian accession year of reckoning. Nebuchadnezzar's first year of reign is 604/603 B.C. Measuring 2520 solar years from 604 B.C. brings us to 1917 A.D. It was on the 9th December 1917 that Jerusalem surrendered to General Allenby's forces. (See Dia. 31 p. 86 Times of the Signs). Adding 70 years to our measuring rod as in other waypoints, we come exactly to the 9th December 1987.

The Intifada

It was on this very day that the Arabs started their stone throwing uprising against Israel; it still continues as I pen these word in July 1990. As one newsletter states:

"Since the commencement of the present 'Intifada', the suffering and consternation of the Israeli people has multiplied greatly. This 'internal war' is the smartest thing the P.L.O. has ever conceived. On so many occasions they have dismally failed to win military victories against the Israeli Defence Force, but at last they have discovered a method by which they can successfully frustrate and hurt Israel. The uprising has been cleverly orchestrated and lavishly financed in order to blacken Israel in the eyes of the world and turn world opinion against her. It is without doubt the most successful campaign they have ever waged and has already done inestimable damage to the image and morale of the Israelis." (Aust. Newsletter I.C.E.J. July '89).

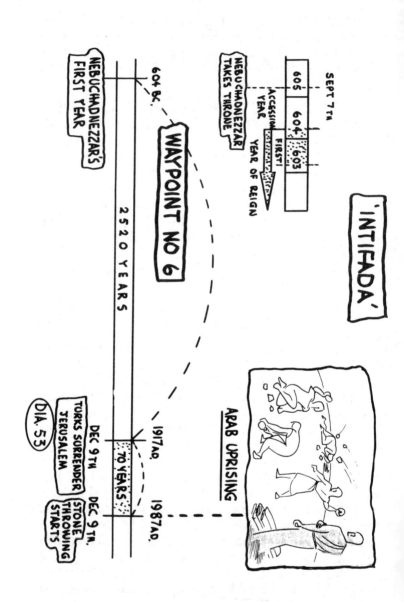

'INTIFADA'

WAYPOINT NO 6

NEBUCHADNEZZAR'S FIRST YEAR

604 B.C.

2520 YEARS

NEBUCHADNEZZAR TAKES THRONE

SEPT 7TH

ACCESSION YEAR

FIRST YEAR

YEAR OF REIGN

605 | 604 | 603

DIA. 53

TURKS SURRENDER JERUSALEM

DEC 9TH

1917 A.D.

70 YEARS

STONE THROWING STARTS

DEC 9TH

1987 A.D.

ARAB UPRISING

Space Satellite (Dia. No. 54)

Nebuchadnezzar came to the throne in September 605 B.C. His first year of reign after the accession year ends in September 603 B.C. If we measure from this date, fully extending our measuring rod 2590 years we come to September 1988 A.D.!

In that month Israel launched an orbital space satellite, making them the only space power in the Middle East. This achievement greatly enhances Israel's military capabilities in the face of Arab hostility.

P.L.O.'s Recognition of Israel

In December 1988 the Palestinian Liberation Organisation, after years of bitter terrorism, finally recognised Israel's right to exist in peace and security. They accepted United Nations Resolutions 242 and 338 as the basis for negotiations to end the Arab-Israel conflict.

Thus in the space of one year from December 9th 1987 to December 14th 1988 we have three key chrono-prophetic developments dating back on the biblical measuring rod of 2590 years (2520 + 70) to the time when Nebuchadnezzar became King of Babylon.

Think of the marvels of this waypoint.
It points to the VERY DAY:-
DECEMBER 9th 1989 'INTIFADA'
It points to the VERY MONTH:-
SEPTEMBER 1988 'ORBITAL SPACE SATELLITE'
It points to the VERY YEAR:-
1988 'P.L.O. RECOGNISE ISRAEL'

*"There is no wisdom, no
    insight, no plan
that can succeed against
    the Lord"* (Proverbs 21:30 NIV)

*"Praise be to the Lord God, the
    God of Israel,*

who alone does marvellous
    deeds.
Praise be to His glorious name
    forever;
May the whole earth be filled
    with His glory.
Amen and Amen'' (Psalm 72:18-19 NIV)

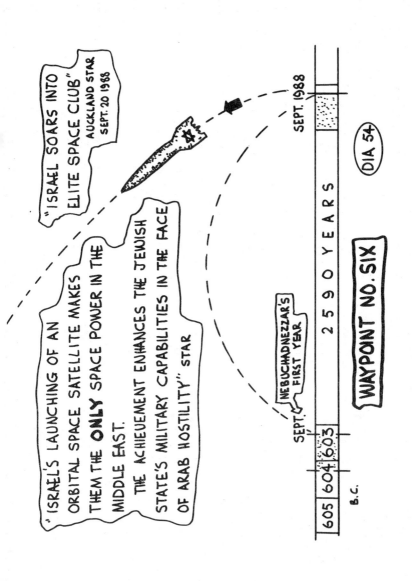

"ISRAEL SOARS INTO ELITE SPACE CLUB" AUCKLAND STAR SEPT. 20 1988

"ISRAEL'S LAUNCHING OF AN ORBITAL SPACE SATELLITE MAKES THEM THE **ONLY** SPACE POWER IN THE MIDDLE EAST.

THE ACHIEVEMENT ENHANCES THE JEWISH STATE'S MILITARY CAPABILITIES IN THE FACE OF ARAB HOSTILITY" STAR

SEPT. 1988

NEBUCHADNEZZAR'S FIRST YEAR

SEPT.

605 604 603

B.C.

2 5 9 0 Y E A R S

WAYPOINT NO. SIX

DIA 54

Select Bibliography

These books are in addition to those referred to in "Times of the Signs" (pgs. 221-224).

Arthur Bedford*	Scripture Chronology	1730 A.D.
Arthur Custance	Hidden Things of God's Revelation	Academic Books 1977
J.B. Dimbleby	The Date of Creation	E. Nisten Ltd 1902
F.W.Grant	The Numerical Structure of Scripture	Loizeaux Bros. 1887
Paul Johnson	A History of the Jews	Weidenfeld & Nicolson 1987
Le Baron W. Kinney	The Greatest Things in the Universe	Loizeaux Bros. 1939
Hal Lindsey	The Road to Holocaust	Bantam Books 1989
Elwood McQuaid	...It Is No Dream	Friends of Israel 1978

*It is astounding that this book published in 1730 (261 years ago!) comes up with the date, 444 B.C. for the decree of Artaxerxes to Nehemiah to rebuild the City of Jerusalem (Nehemiah 2:1-8).
Also the 3rd April 33 A.D. for the day Christ was crucified.
These dates are the same as the latest research. Refer:
1. Chronological Aspects of the Life of Christ, H.W. Hoechner (Zondervan).
2. 'Nature' Vol. 306 22 Dec. 1983 entitled 'Dating the Crucifixion.' 'Nature' is the elite British scientific journal.

The author can be reached at this address:-
G.T. CURLE
5A PARAU ST
MT. ROSKILL
AUCKLAND 4
NEW ZEALAND